On the Motives which led Husserl to Transcendental Idealism

PHAENOMENOLOGICA

COLLECTION FONDÉE PAR H. L. VAN BREDA ET PUBLIÉE SOUS LE
PATRONAGE DES CENTRES D'ARCHIVES-HUSSERL

64

ROMAN INGARDEN

On the Motives which led Husserl to Transcendental Idealism

Translated from the Polish by
ARNÓR HANNIBALSSON

ROMAN INGARDEN

On the Motives which led Husserl to Transcendental Idealism

Translated from the Polish by
ARNÓR HANNIBALSSON PH. D.

MARTINUS NIJHOFF / DEN HAAG / 1975

Translated from the Polish "O motywach, które doprowadziły Husserla do transcendentalnego idealizmu" from *Z badań nad filozofią współczesną* /Dzieła Filozoficzne, pp. 550–622
© by Państwowe Wydawnictwo Naukowe, Warszawa 1963

ISBN 90 247 1751 5

PRINTED IN THE NETHERLANDS

McCormick Theological Seminary LIBRARY

4721

Ingarden, Roman, 1893-

On the motives which led Husserl to transcendentalism.

X The Hague   Nijhoff

1975

(Phaenomenologica; 64)

NO. OF COPIES   SOURCE OF INFORMATION 90-247-1751-5

DEALER Nijhoff-co-7-30-62

DATE 12-10-75 EST. PRICE   FUND   INV. DATE 10-30-79 EST 15.00

TABLE OF CONTENTS

TRANSLATOR'S PREFACE

Roman Ingarden studied under Husserl before and during the first world war. He belonged to the so-called Göttingen group of Husserl's pupils. Husserl's doctrine was accepted by them and interpreted in a realist vein. Ingarden defended this view all his life. He opposed the development of phenomenology towards idealism. A considerable part of Ingarden's great creative effort is dedicated to the construction of a realist phenomenology and thus, according to him, to continuing the erection of the theoretical structure whose foundations were laid by Husserl in his *Logical Investigations*. From Ingarden's standpoint the question of idealism versus realism was a crucial one. Ingarden published several studies on Husserl. The first one was written in 1918 and the last one was published posthumously. The present essay was printed in Ingarden's book Z badań nad filozofią współczesną (Inquiries into Contemporary Philosophy 1963) along with a number of other essays on Husserl and his philosophy. This one is representative for Ingarden's positions. It is a good example of his contribution to an important controversy in the history of phenomenology, and it gives the reader an idea of Ingarden's critique of Husserlian idealism against the background of his argument for realism.

Thanks and acknowledgements are due to Mr. J. E. Llewelyn of Edinburgh University. This translation was undertaken in collaboration with him.

Arnór Hannibalsson

Kópavogur, Iceland
21.II.1975

INTRODUCTION

I have often asked myself why Husserl, really, headed in the direction of transcendental idealism from the time of his *Ideas*[1] whereas at the time of the *Logical Investigations* he clearly occupied a realist position. In later years he at last reached a solution whose correctness he could not doubt.

For everyone who knows Husserl's methods of work it will not be surprising that various arguments emerging from his investigations should move him in this direction. For a long time Husserl worked on a certain set of problems which he elaborated according to his interests at the time without being explicitly conscious of the broad connections between them. Only as the years went by did there begin to emerge a certain unified pattern of philosophi-

---

[1] *Ideas I* is known to have been published in the spring of 1913; there is no clear evidence as to when it was written. In 1950 a fragment of Husserl's lectures from the spring of 1907 was published (under the title *Die Idee der Phänomenologie, Fünf Vorlesungen*, editor Walter Biemel). The editor thinks that at that time Husserl had already adopted transcendental idealism. However, it is only possible to assert that Husserl reached the concept of transcendental phenomenology at this time and in these lectures outlined for the first time, if only roughly by comparison with the version to appear in *Ideas I*, the notion of the phenomenological reduction. Undoubtedly, he became conscious at that time of the problems of constitution, as can be seen from the *Lectures on the Phenomenology of Internal Time Consciousness*, previously published. Neither the inclusion of these problems in the agenda nor the results of constitutive investigations in the above-mentioned works included a solution favorable to transcendental idealism as it appears clearly and undoubtedly in the *Cartesian Meditations* and the *Formal and Transcendental Logic*. The fundamental concept of this logic belongs to the beginning of the twenties; only from that time does Husserl hold a crystallized and firm position in this matter. When I talked with Husserl almost daily in September and October 1927 it became clear to me that Husserl had reached a final decision and that the situation had changed radically in comparison with the state of affairs very well known to me in my student years at Göttingen and later in Freiburg. At that time Husserl was at least sensitive to arguments against idealism but he himself did not hold a uniform position. The transition to idealism was a process that took more than ten years, and this was to be expected as it was carried out in many new analytical investigations to which Husserl gave no systematic order.

cal problems which Husserl tried to grasp either from a single methodological point of view or by studying the clusters of problems themselves and the relations between them. The totality of this set of problems reached at once in Husserl's eyes such vast dimensions that a single person could not be expected to solve them. Husserl makes many attempts to draw up the outlines of this totality but – in spite of all his efforts – he has to be contented with more or less detailed sketches of parts of it. After he had worked out each of them there followed usually long periods of physical exhaustion and during these periods he never succeeded in organizing any work of great dimensions. These fragments are elaborated in various periods of Husserl's life and differed from each other in various details and crystallized themselves around different central problems or fundamental theses. When we look now at the whole of Husserl's investigations (which are now known to us) it appears necessary to make distinctions between different groups of motives or arguments which, in the last resort, result in transcendental idealism whose total picture is, perhaps, painted most carefully in *Formal and Transcendental Logic* and in the *Cartesian Meditations*[2] but which is nevertheless never finally substantiated by Husserl. It will be useful to isolate these groups of arguments or motives which led Husserl to transcendental idealism. It will be of help for a critical consideration of the foundations of his solution. These groups are, to mention only the most important ones, as follows:

1. Assertions regarding Husserl's concept of philosophy as rigorous science.
2. Postulates defining the right method of the theory of knowledge.
3. Positive results of the analysis of outer perception of material objects and also the so-called constitutive analysis.
4. Some fundamental assertions regarding formal ontology.

[2] These *Meditations* are known to have been occasioned by external circumstances, an invitation to lecture in Paris. Husserl was not satisfied with them. For many years after they were published in a French translation Husserl intended to publish them in German and worked on a new version which, as he wrote to me in a letter, was to become his main work. This work was to contain the elaboration of the totality ot problems and tundamental theses of transcendental phenomenology. Unfortunately, this plan was never realized. Husserl worked on a new project for a number of years later to be entitled *Die Krisis der europäischen Wissenschaften und die transzendentale Phänomenologie,* and this too was occasioned by external circumstances. Husserl never finished this work.

Before discussing these assertions and their role in the argument for transcendental idealism it may be useful to make clear whether and to what extent it is possible to argue for the view that Husserl was a realist during the period of his *Logical Investigations*. I begin my deliberations by looking into this matter.

PART I

HUSSERL'S POSITION

I. THE ORIGINAL REALIST STANDPOINT

Some are of the opinion that there never was such a period in which Husserl was a realist with regard to the real world and that only certain of his Göttingen pupils interpreted Husserl's opinions realistically.[1] These were the pupils from the period before the first world war influenced by A. Reinach who was originally Th. Lipps's pupil and was brought up in the Munich group of phenomenologists who adopted a definitely realist point of view.

In all this, one thing is undoubtedly true: in Husserl's published work before the *Ideas* there is not one devoted to the question of the existence of the world and there are not even any arguments on this subject. There are no clearly formulated assertions about the real world which could be interpreted in the spirit of a realism of one type or another. Husserl did not involve himself in this problem in his work published before 1913. From this it does not follow that it is not possible to arrive indirectly at an understanding of what his position was implicitly or potentially. It will be instructive – maybe unexpectedly – to take Husserl's attitude to the concept of truth as expounded in the first volume of *Logical Investigations*. This concept underwent a substantial change in

---

[1] This view of the first period of Husserl's philosophy is held by some of the collaborators of the Husserl Archives in Louvain, first and foremost by H. van Breda†. They quote various manuscripts by Husserl, unpublished and inaccessible outside Louvain. But neither van Breda nor any of the Archives' collaborators were Husserl's direct pupils or knew him personally with the exception of Landgrebe and Fink who did not work in Louvain after the second world war. H. van Breda appeared on the recommendation of his professor Noël in Freiburg in the autumn of 1938 when Husserl was no longer alive. It is to his merit that he rescued Husserl's manuscripts and transferred them to Louvain along with Husserl's library.

Formal and Transcendental Logic but this change stands in close connection with a change in his understanding of the being of the real world. The controversy between realists and idealists concerning the existence of the real world is not about the question whether the real world, the material world in particular, exists in general (even Berkeley would protest energetically if somebody told him that he affirmed the non-existence of the material world), but about the mode of the world's existence and what its existential relation is to acts of consciousness in which objects belonging to this world are cognized. Husserl – not having yet at his disposal the distinctions between modes and moments of existence which I tried to introduce in the *Controversy about the Existence of the World*[2] – uses in looking at this matter certain traditional terms which are equivocal and not very clear but such that it is possible to surmise what he really means. From the positions of his later idealism Husserl protests against the "absolutization" of the real world. This means that the existence which is only "for" the conscious subject and does not possess its own essence is not to be considered as a being "in itself" which is endowed with its own effective essence. This "in itself" (*an sich*) is then something which belongs to the real world if it is considered "absolutized" or, in other words, such as we all consider it in everyday practice when we – as Husserl says in the *Ideas* – take up the natural attitude. If the world was "in itself," i.e. existed unrelated to its cognition by anybody and had its own determination "itself for itself" included in itself and unequivocally defined, then there must be a certain understanding of the truth both of categorical judgments in the logical sense and of the cognition of objects concerning this world. If there is no such being and it is only possible to agree upon a certain existence "for somebody" either experiencing or cognizing, then the concept of truthfulness of cognitive results must be changed radically as far as it is then possible to speak in any reasonable sense about "truthfulness." At the end of the first volume, in the chapter called "The Idea of Pure Logic," of the *Logical Investigations* Husserl writes as follows:

"Two meanings can be attached to this objective interconnection which ideally pervades scientific thought, and which gives

[2] Cf. *ibidem*, Chapter III and sect. 31.

"unity" to such thought, and so to science as such: it can be understood as an interconnection of the things to which our thought-experiences (actual or possible) are intentionally directed, or, on the other hand, as an interconnection of truths, in which this unity of things comes to count objectively as being what it is. These two things are given together *a priori*, and are mutually inseparable. Nothing can be without being thus or thus determined, and that it is thus and thus determined, is the self-subsistent truth which is the necessary correlate of the self-subsistent being. What holds of single truths, or single states of affairs, plainly also holds of interconnections of truths or of states of affairs. This self-evident inseparability is not, however, identity. In these truths or interconnections of truths the actual existence of things and of interconnections of things finds expression. But the interconnections of truths differ from the interconnections of things, which are "truly" in the former; this at once appears in the fact that truths which hold of truths do not coincide with truths that hold of the things posited in such truths."[3]

In order to make the matter sufficiently clear and to avoid misunderstanding Husserl emphasizes that he uses the words "object," "thing" in such a wide sense that they mean both something real and something ideal, i.e. both a thing (*Ding*) or a process and a certain *species* or mathematical relation or being as what ought to be.[4]

As can be seen from the quoted text, Husserl understands being, and that means any being, real or ideal, as something which is in itself determined in one or another way, more exactly: as what contains this determination in itself and what is true corresponds to this being and is determined in itself: it is what it is and it is such as it is. Each has to be understood as something which is in itself and is such as it is and only *idealiter* coordinated with itself. This is to be seen from the observation that what is, the object, the thing, is to be understood in the widest possible sense to cover both what is real and what is ideal, and it is also to be seen from the thesis which Husserl argues for in the *Logical Investiga-*

---

3 Cf. *l.c.*, p. 228. (English translation, vol. I, p. 225–226).
4 Cf. *l.c.*, p. 225 ff.

tions that logical formations, concepts (meanings), sentences, theories are ideal objects.

It can be doubted whether Husserl opposes "truths in themselves" and "things in themselves" in a satisfactory way. These truths, according to their description, seem to be rather states of affairs taking place in things rather than logical formations, i.e. certain linguistic formations having a certain meaning which stand for either things or states of affairs. Nevertheless, Husserl's mode of dealing with what exists as what is and is in itself such or otherwise cannot be doubted. Neither can it be doubted that the view expounded by him on this matter in the *Formal and Transcendental Logic* is different, as he denies that this "in itself" (*an sich*) belongs to logical formations and the real. It must be doubted, however, whether Husserl himself clearly realized this difference and whether the quotation from *Logical Investigations* can be interpreted in such a way which would support the attitude taken in the *Logic*. There is written and, seemingly, also oral evidence that Husserl saw clearly that he changed his view in *Logical Investigations*. Such evidence can be found in Husserl's letter to me of the 5th of April 1918 quoted by me in the essay *The Main Lines of Development of Husserl's Philosophy*.

From the quoted text it can be seen that my understanding of logical formations which I emphasize ("*Wahrheiten an sich*") as "states of affairs" is an incidental mistake of formulation and that Husserl clearly treats sentences or "judgments" in the logical sense as linguistic formations imbued with meaning but not as something taking place in things themselves. Furthermore, it can be clearly seen that Husserl stresses that he considers his view on logical formations as being ideal objects to be false and that he changed his opinion. But it can be doubted if this embraces also the concept of objects or things "in themselves." The last sentence of the quoted text clearly shows that the problems lead to the problem of constitution and the analysis of primary time consciousness and in the consequent sentence – not quoted – Husserl writes clearly that he actually attacks the analysis of time constitution in primary consciousness.[5]

---

[5] It became apparent later that these investigations were included in a manuscript created in the year 1918 in Bernau. It remains unpublished. In the course of their further development they lead finally to the position which Husserl occupies in

The "oral" evidence that Husserl considered his position in *Prolegomena* to be false is his words in a conversation with me in the autumn of 1927. When he asked what was the subject of my tutorials at the University of Lwów I told him that in one of the tutorials I read, among other things, the first volume of the *Logical Investigations*, especially the last chapter. Husserl said: "Ach, warum haben sie dies gelesen, da habe ich mich so verrannt." ("Oh, why did you read that. I was so wrong there.") This was a clear expression of disapproval of the view taken there.

I think that on this basis I am justified in saying that in the period of *Logical Investigations* Husserl took the "realist" view in relation to real objects as it is set forth above and that he later abandoned it as being false.

It is evident that what I said a moment ago concerns only one point of the complicated problem of "idealism-realism," but a decisive one and sufficient for characterizing Husserl's position in the period considered.

I am now going to discuss particular assertions, made by Husserl, which can be treated as arguments for the final solution in the spirit of transcendental idealism. I express myself cautiously by saying "can be treated" as such arguments, since Husserl does not develop such arguments and does not rely expressis verbis on such arguments. Although they can be discovered in Husserl's texts they were not used by him in this logical function. This fact is connected with Husserl's general style of work which is not a logical construction of thought but rather reports about descriptive investigations on the nature or essence of certain objects or facts.

2. THE CONCEPT OF PHILOSOPHY
AS RIGOROUS SCIENCE

The concept of philosophy as rigorous science[6] emerged in close relation to Husserl's critical attitude to European philosophy in its factual form. Husserl, who came over to philosophy from

Cartesian Meditations and *Formal and Transcendental Logic*, i.e. to the transcendental idealist position in the Husserlian sense. At the moment when Husserl wrote his letter to me the matter was insufficiently clarified by Husserl himself who worked intensively on these problems at that time.

[6] Cf. *Philosophie als strenge Wissenschaft*, Logos, vol. I, 1911.

mathematics, condemned not only the many existing philosophies but also – as he said – the unending "quarrels" (*Hader*) between philosophers but first and foremost the mode of philosophizing inside each system with the help of undefined fundamental concepts, the assertion of theorems without demonstration, the tendency to construct systems as closed theoretical entities without taking any care of their relation to reality and so on. All these problems made impossible the reconciliation of different trends and the discovery of a firm foundation for philosophy. Husserl fought all his life for this firm foundation,[7] for clarity, for distinction between all that was frequently rather carelessly confused. But above all he fought for responsibility in philosophical research and devoted many years to the elaboration of a method which, according to him, was to secure for philosophy the status of a science. It is maybe unexpected and surprising that Husserl who was trained as a mathematician did not seek salvation for philosophy in the mathematical method which had from time to time stood out like a beacon as an ideal worthy of imitation by philosophers. But mathematical logic could not satisfy him. Husserl is known to have occupied himself with it in the nineties of the last century and it prevented many sceptics from seeing any scientific value in philosophy. Just where Husserl demanded clarity and understanding mathematical logicians were satisfied with conventionalistic solutions and relatively shallow scepticism which finally, as we know, led to radical formalism and physicalism in the interpretation of logical formations. In the controversy about the foundations of mathematics at the beginning of this century and later the search for understanding of and insight into the indefinable structure of logical formations, the apprehension of the ultimate grounds for the validity of axioms became something which people excluded from their agenda claiming to know that nothing "scientific" can be said in these matters. These were the points which – according to Husserl who was in the period of the *Logical Investigations* defending the existence of one unique and ultimately demonstrated truth – were to be finally clarified by insight and understanding. The exactness of mathematics was, maybe, for Husserl at that time a certain ideal worthy of esteem

---

[7] In German "fester Boden." This is the expression which Husserl often used in his lectures and private conversations.

but in its foundation and realization it was not worthy of imitation as a methodological model. The method of phenomenological analysis was used by Husserl for many years but he did not see its essential sense and efficiency clearly enough – even after the publication of the *Logical Investigations*. In the first edition of this work he described phenomenology as "descriptive psychology" in the sense of Brentano.[8] Prior to his final elaboration of the idea of phenomenology it was essential for the later formation of phenomenology as "transcendental" philosophy in the period of the search for "rigorous science" to emphasize the acquisition in philosophy of a "firm foundation." By a "firm" foundation (strong) is meant an unshakeable one. The same can be said in the characteristic way for the theory of knowledge: a cognition must be gained in philosophy which cannot be doubted but is "absolute" in its validity and certainty. To discover a cognition of this kind and at the same time to construct a method which would guarantee its acquisition and its use – this was the ideal and aim which followed from the postulate of philosophy as "rigorous" science. The *maximum*, or better *optimum*, cognition available to Husserl from the point of view of the *Logical Investigations* was "ideation," i.e. a mode of knowing what is ideal, the so-called species. But with its help – as somebody said maliciously – Husserl could only organize "hunting for *species*," i.e. gain a foundation for an aprioristic science such as mathematics. But if philosophy is to be taken in general is it then possible to construct it with the help of "ideation"?

We know that Husserl in the first decade of the 20th century widened essentially the horizon of his interests beyond the problem group of the *Logical Investigations* on the one hand in the direction of problems of epistemology, which he had not delved into until then, mainly problems of outer sense perception, and on the other hand in the direction of problems concerning the objects

---

[8] It is not quite clear what Brentano himself understood by "descriptive psychology," especially in the period when Husserl listened to his lectures in Vienna. Oskar Kraus, the editor of a new edition of *Psychologie vom empirischen Standpunkt* pays attention to this problem in his Introduction which, if his remarks were true, would bring together Brentano's descriptive psychology and Husserl's phenomenology. It has to be remembered that Kraus wrote this when the idea of phenomenology was already crystallized and phenomenology was flourishing and it was commonly said by the Brentanists that Brentano knew before Husserl everything that the latter later asserted.

of the real world, especially, as it is usually expressed since Kant,[9] problems concerning the form of the world, time and space. In these investigations it very soon became evident that outer perception could not yield indubitable cognition. The question then arose if such cognition could be found in inner or, more exactly, immanent perception. This thought must have occurred to Husserl, he was, after all, Brentano's pupil and he introduced the concept of "inner conciousness": by means of it a cognition was to be gained which could not be doubted. Thereby it was suggested that immanent perception was to be analyzed and its cognitive value to be discovered. Reaching a solution on this matter was the decisive step in the direction of the so-called "final subjectivity." By invoking the help of "eidetic" cognition it was relatively easy to reach the idea of pure transcendental phenomenology which through its appeal to the final subjectivity of pure consciousness was to discover not only the final source of all knowledge of the real world but also by a simple transposition of the problem complex such as has often been made in the past was to make possible a deduction of the real world from the ultimate source of pure consciousness. In that way the purely methodological ideal of philosophy as rigorous science whose results would be indubitable and undoubted prepared the ground for a transition to an essentially metaphysical solution, to transcendental idealism (whose metaphysicality was, as a matter of fact, not evident).

3. POSTULATES DETERMINING THE APPROPRIATE METHOD OF EPISTEMOLOGY

It so happened that in the very years that Husserl jumped into the arena of epistemology, Leonard Nelson directed a sharp attack against the theory of knowledge.[10] We know that Nelson made an attempt to show the impossibility of epistemology by pointing out that inevitably in it one cannot avoid committing

---

[9] But Husserl does not use this expression.

[10] Cf. Leonard Nelson, *Über das sogenannte Erkenntnisproblem. Die Unmöglichkeit der Erkenntnistheorie*, vol. III, Abhandlungen der Friesschen Schule, also in the Acts of the IV International Congress of Philosophy, 1911. Husserl's ideas must have been completely crystallized in this period. Nelson was a *Dozent* in Göttingen from the year 1909.

the error of *petitio principii*. Husserl, as far as I know, never spoke
nor wrote about this opinion expressed by Nelson and must have
seen this danger clearly for himself, but he certainly knew about
Nelson's book. Whatever the relations were between the two
thinkers, it is a fact that in the period when I heard Husserl's
lectures (with interruptions, from 1912 to 1917) he very often
drew attention in his lectures and seminars to the "nonsense"
(*Widersinn*) in the attempt to arrive at an epistemological solution, e.g. concerning the cognitive value of outer perception, by
appealing to the existence of qualities in objects given in cognition
of the kind which is investigated when, e.g. – as was usual in the
psycho-physiology of the second half of the 19th century – we
appeal to "physical stimuli" which act upon what is called our
senses in order to show that sense perception falsely informs us
about "secondary" qualities of material objects. It is also a fact
that the application of the phenomenological reduction, which
Husserl introduced with another aim in mind in *Ideas I, eo ipso*
removes the danger of *petitio principii* in the investigations into
the experiential mode of cognition of the objects of the real world.
After having carried out this reduction we find ourselves, nevertheless, *ipso facto* in the area of pure transcendental consciousness
inside which we are to carry out all epistemological investigations; but, in addition, it has to be agreed that every being (real
or ideal or purely intentional) is to be deduced from the essence of
the operations (acts) of pure consciousness. It seems to be that
from the point of view of a valid epistemological methodology a certain kind of priority is to be demanded for pure consciousness, and
that this is possible is also shown by the theory of immanent
perception and the results of the analysis of primary constitutive
consciousness constituting, for example, time. But, along with this,
this "priority" of pure consciousness begins to assume a metaphysical character in the form even of a thesis of the absolute
existence of pure consciousness, on the one hand, and, on the
other hand, of an existential dependence of all other being, and,
above all, of the real world, on pure consciousness. The danger of
petitio principii in epistemology is removed by the phenomenological reduction but it leads to an account of the existence of the
world which (in spite of all differences, from, for example,
Berkeley's position, which Husserl himself constantly and em-

phatically stressed) comes alarmingly close to the Marburgian neokantism, of which Husserl was often accused on the grounds of similarities between his *Ideas* and Natorp's *Allgemeine Psychologie* of 1912.

4. THE RESULTS OF THE INVESTIGATIONS INTO OUTER PERCEPTION AND THE CONSTITUTIVE ANALYSIS OF OBJECTS OF THE REAL WORLD

It is undoubtedly possible to hold that the position of transcendental idealism is not reached simply by using phenomenological reduction and by avoiding the error of *petitio principii* in epistemology. Sometimes it seems that even using this reduction it is possible to avoid the idealist solution but this solution is adopted only because, in carrying out the analysis of outer perception and the constitutive analysis (*Betrachtung*) certain decisions are made about various substantial matters that lead unavoidably to transcendental idealism in relation to the external world and even in relation to all transcendent objects.

We would expect that in these investigations some epistemological solutions would be reached on the basis of which the old controversy between idealism and realism would be solved and that Husserl would succeed in this. Husserl analyzed outer (sense) perception so carefully from all possible angles that he obtained results which no empirical or positivistic trend can boast of, although these schools were to have great successes in this field according to their position and programme. Husserl also studied different general structures of pure consciousness in such a penetrating and subtle way and gained so many convincing results in this area that he could be expected to reach the essential facts leading to a solution.

And, really, we find in his works from the times of *Ideas I* several statements which play a role in all this controversy but which are, at the same time, arguments for "idealism" although Husserl does not characterize them as such. I shall point out some of them which have an epistemological character.

a) Objects (things, processes) given in outer perception are

"transcendent" in relation to it, i.e. they do not enter into experience of perception itself.[11] It follows that the thing given in
this perception might not exist although the same perceptual
experience took place as that through which it (the thing) is given
in a bodily fashion to the perceiving subject. Non-existence of
this object would not change anything; it would escape the
attention of the subject not accidentally but because of the
essence of the structure of outer experience and of what is given
in it.[1] On the other hand, the perceptual experience itself given
in immanent perception creates with it an unmediated unity[13]
and from its occurrence follows the impossibility of the non-
existence of perceptual experience and thereby the impossibility
of removing or undermining the thesis of its existence.[14]

b) Every particular outer perception (e.g. seeing) is in its essence
"partial" (in parts) and not adequate to what is given in it. It is
one-sided and partial apprehension of the perceived object and
the "other side" – which is turned away from the perceiving
subject – and the interior of the thing is only co-given or co-meant
(the thing is given intuitively (seen) and, characteristically, has
an "other" side and is determined in a certain way – with a certain
form, color etc. – and a certain determined "interior"). Only in
the further course of the experience (encounter), i.e. in other
perceptions of "the same" thing can the back become the front
and then it is given effectively, *explicitly*. We can also in certain
cases "peep" into the "interior" – by cutting or making the thing
transparant etc. These later perceptions of the same thing can
corroborate the result of the actual perception but that is not
necessary. It can happen that what was co-meant or co-given was

---

11 Cf. *Ideas I*, p. 73 (first edition).

12 In another passage in *Ideas I* Husserl acknowledges that as a result of the non-
existence of a perceived object the perception itself would change essentially but
would not cease to exist. I think that this is not a contradiction in his position but
that Husserl has in mind other cases of perception, especially those in which we convince ourselves that an object which we, e.g., expected to find in a certain place does
not exist and its non-existence is shown somehow in perception itself.

13 "Eine unvermittelte Einheit," cf. *l.c.*, p. 68.

14 It is not obvious whether the character of this argument is epistemological or
ontological. It relies on the s t r u c t u r e of experiences, immanent perception on one
side and transcendent on the other; it can, however, be said that because it is a
structure of c o g n i t i v e experiences then the argument has to be called epistemological.
But this has no great significance.

falsely meant, the thing's back was quite different from what we had thought (and intuitively justified) in the initial perception. This otherness of the thing which we perceive is in this respect always possible but the perspective of further perception cannot virtually exclude the possibility whose foundation lies in the very structure of outer perception. The "back" of a thing may appear at one time as it is co-given but at another time to a certain extent (but not entirely) different. But this is not simply a consequence of the common fact that at one time something happens one way and at an other time another way; it arises necessarily, rather, from the essential structure of "outer" perception itself and, on the other hand, from the essential structure of the spatial thing. If certain parts of this thing did not cover other parts of it then perception would not be in this sense "onesided" or "partial." From the spatiality of the thing (its possession of various parts, its limits in every direction, and from the determination of these limits) and from its non-transparency on the one hand, and, on the other, from the fact that we perceive from a single point of view, it follows necessarily that the thing cannot be given in sense perception (vision) from all sides all at once. That it is "onesided" seems to be, in these circumstances, natural and necessary. It is rather surprising that it is not onesided in a more radical sense, i.e. that in spite of the fact that all seeing is onesided we possess – as it were in spite of reasons for expecting it to be impossible – a certain intuitive knowledge about the "other side" and the "inside" and never see the thing as only "onesided" and as if the "other side" were excluded or left no intuitive trace of itself in our visual experience. It is as though perception here offers something "beyond its capacity," so to speak, as if it gives more than is within its power to give.[15] And just because of this it can be "verified" or "falsified" in other perceptions of the same

---

[15] Genetic psychologists would certainly say that this is so only because when we look at something we see it as having only one side and only imagine that it possesses "another" side, and this imagination is only "association" which is possible because we have seen the thing before from the "other" side. This is a gross oversimplification of the problem in which the truth is that no particular outer perception is quite independent of other perceptions of the same thing but is in its essence a member of a certain set of outer perceptions. This cannot be elaborated here. Whatever the explanation of the facts, spoken about in the text, the essential question is whether and to what extent these facts are important in connection with the controversy between idealism and realism.

thing. Other circumstances explain why these two alternatives are possible. Namely first of all that a thing given in perception is given as another being in relation to perception and existing in itself independently of its being perceived or not. It is given to us, in other words, as existentially autonomous and, particularly, "real." It can have its qualities (back and front) because of its own nature and because it just is, it is somehow in itself and eventually changes as its qualities and its environment determine but not because of the way it is perceived. If it changed itself on account of somebody's perception then a different perception would make it different and it would always be as it was perceived and there would be no possibility of its being other than it was at any moment when it was perceived (from a certain side), and there would be no possibility of verifying or falsifying in another perception what was in a previous one. The thing can, however, present itself in this other perception differently from how it, so to speak, intuitively promises to present itself in the given perception via the qualities appearing explicitly among the data of this perception; and this is connected with another structural characteristic of perceived objects. One assortment of the thing's qualities – the one given explicitly in a certain perception – does not have to indicate univocally all the rest of its qualities; indeed, it does not indicate them at all. The designation does not appear necessarily in the data of the perceived qualities. If it did, i.e. if one assortment of the thing's qualities constantly indicated univocally all the rest of its qualities then there would be no surprise in future experience and it would be useless to refer to future experience. If, however, later experience does sometimes surprise us, this suggests that there is a certain degree of looseness in the structure of the perceived object which allows for the possibilities of its changing or simply being something other than what we thought it was. These possibilities are guaranteed by the fact that a given perceptual experience is consistent with a set of qualities of the thing.

If, however, we suppose that there may be changes in the perceived object in the period of time which divides one perception from the others, then the verification of an actual perception of a certain thing with the help of other perceptions becomes very difficult if not entirely impossible. It is not known, then, whether at the moment of perceiving this thing in the past it truly had a certain attribute x among the attributes belonging to the part turned away from the viewer and in the period of time which divides it from a new perception it changed so that it does not possess the attribute x any more and therefore would not show it *explicitly* in a new perception, or, the other way, whether it did not change in the given period of time and did not possess the attribute x during the first perception but only an illusion led to the attribute's being intuitively ascribed to it. In this situation it is no longer known what the perceived thing really is in all these respects which transcend what is effectively given in a given perception. On the other hand, knowledge gained with the help of outer perceptions becomes not only onesided and inadequate but, further, of necessity characterized by an uncertainty which cannot be removed by referring to other perceptions of the same thing.

But the looseness of the structure of a perceived thing is not necessarily so complete that no given attribute indicates any of the remaining ones. We will soon become convinced of that.

c) Against what the English empiricists once asserted, in outer perception not only how the thing we perceive is given, but also what the thing is. We see not only "something" brown and bulky etc. but we see a brown wardrobe, a wooden table, a rocky mountain etc. Naturally, this does not apply to cases in which perception is so lacking in sharpness and clarity that in having it we do not know what we are dealing with. E.g. if we are driving a car at night we may not distinguish clearly whether what we see in the dark is a pedestrian or a cyclist or something else. But these are exceptional cases which we try to explain by referring to other perceptions. And we seek them until it becomes clear what kind of object it is. Sometimes the perception is clear, i.e. many different attributes of the object seen stand out sharply but, nevertheless, we do not know precisely what it is, especially if it has a specific nature. We see e.g. the general nature of a thing, e.g. we see a tree, but it is not given that this is specifically an oak (e.g. a coniferous Japanese oak). I do not know, yet, what it is. It is essential, however, that in the course of experiences relating to a certain thing we can reach such a stage of knowledge in which the "whatness' of the given object becomes not only known to us but is, moreover, intuitively given in perception. In limiting cases even the whatness of individual objects in their specificity and singleness is given. This is so e.g. when we perceive a certain determinate person whose specific physiognomy is given clearly to us in spite of a wide variety of changes among the attributes perceived.

There are close connections and interrelationships between the "whatness" of an object (its individual or general nature) and determinations deciding h o w it is. If we are first given the "what" of an object then its *how* is not, as a matter of fact, in every respect univocally fixed. For it may be, at least usually, such or otherwise in certain respects; however, the variability of some of its "properties" is not unlimited but usually precisely determined. As soon as the limits of variability are crossed the nature of the object is destroyed and therewith the object itself for its individual nature is destroyed. Husserl used to say that the object then "exploded." Expressing this phenomenologically, we say that depending upon what qualitative determinations of a certain thing are given in perception it (the thing) presents itself to us *sub specie* of a certain determined "what." We can never exclude the possibility that future perceptions of "the same" thing will show it to us in such variable qualitative determinations (attributes) that its "what" becomes violated or also – if we may so put it – that there occurs a jump into quite another "what" such that either the given thing ceases to be given at all or it appears that its "what" is quite different from what it initially seemed to be its nature on the basis of previous series of perceptions. Hence it is in principle doubtful exactly what the nature ("what") of the things we perceive is, whether it is such as it later seems to be or somehow otherwise. It remains always theoretically doubtful if what "hereto" is given in outer perception exists in reality at all or if in its place there exists something else or nothing at all. It becomes doubtful in general if there exists some "what" and some "such" in the thing itself or, on the contrary, whether this "what" of the thing appearing in perception is only a certain (indicated by the previous course of experience) synthetic phenomenon of such a "what" and relative to the given set of perceptions; i.e. whether it is only a c o r r e l a t e of a definite set of perceptions, something which exists only f o r these perceptions (or also for the subjects possessing such perceptions), and is nothing "in itself" and in particular nothing in the thing in itself. A doubt can be raised whether the notion of such an "in itself" with a nature of its own and qualification of the object founded in the thing itself is not a principally erroneous thought which is to be replaced by the thought that every thing is "for the subject" possessing certain perceptions and is nothing "in itself." Thus we find ourselves again at the gates of idealism.

d) To every object which can be given at all in perception there belongs in principle an infinite set of possible perceptions in which it is or could be given if a real perception occurred. In practice, this set can never be exhausted because it is infinite. Nevertheless, only after it was completely exhausted would a final and certain determination of the essence, nature ("what") be reached and only then could one establish the existence of what is given in these perceptions (e.g. a certain specific thing). Because of the nature of outer perception (which is always one-sided) we have to bear in mind that new perceptions not yet experienced may introduce some modification in the thing's previous determination, a modification which could not only supplement its determination but at the same time alter the determination of the object arising from "previous" experience. Every absolute ascription (in the form of a simple categorical assertion) of a certain nature or a certain quality (determining the "how" of the object) to what is given in perception is basically unjustified. It is a violation, if I may so put it, of the limits of validity (*Geltung*) prescribed by a closed set of earlier experiences. Ascriptions regarding what is perceived[16] may be made only if qualified as "according to previous experience" and "so long as nothing to the contrary occurs in future experience." Nevertheless, only if it is possible to drop this reservation, only if – supposing the expression be allowed – this kind of violation is permitted is it in principle possible to say that "being in itself" of what is real is directly accessible only through perception.[17]

---

[16] Evidently, only outer perception is meant here or, more generally, perception of transcendent objects, but I omit this addition in order to avoid repetition.

[17] I add "directly" as what is real is evidently cognitively accessible to us in the corresponding operations of thought, i.e. in such operations in which the object is not given to us in the original or presented intuitively. It can be said, accordingly, that in

If we remain within the limits of a closed series of experiences and if we observe exactly the limits of its validity then it is permitted to speak about a thing (or more generally an object) exclusively only as corresponding to the closed set of perceptions, i.e. as what is intentionally designated by those and only those perceptions. The postulate – which, it seems, is epistemologically firmly proved – of using our assertions exactly in the field of cognitive effectiveness of the given mode of cognition, dictates the need to remain inside these limits. Then, strictly speaking, the things given in outer perception are only intentional correlates of perceptions, phenomena. They are something "for" the subject possessing the perceptions in question but nothing "in itself" although they seem to be such in particular perceptions.

e) Suppose the objective sense (*sens przedmiotowy, Gegenstands-sinn*) achieved in a certain deliberate set of perceptions[18] (the "what" and the sense of particular determinations as to the "how" of this object) is a synthetic result of an already acquired set of perceptions of it and that, besides, it is not permissible to speak of what is "in itself" (as shown in the last section), with other words, what is its own being and the determination of the per-ceived object, in particular of a thing. It will then be easy to regard this synthetic result as a "creation" of the set of percep-tions concerned and to state that it "constitutes" itself in the course of experience and becomes "founded" (u s t a n o w i o n y).[19]

consequence of this reservation the sentence just asserted is a tautology, i.e. that it says that what is real is perceptually accessible only through perception. But the concept of "direct cognitive access" is in its content not identical with the concept "perceivability." The first one says only that the object is to be intuitively presented in the flesh to the cognizing subject, the second that this is to be done in a certain way. It is not thereby asserted, as many empirically oriented readers might hold, that this way was to be "empirical," namely, the result of physical stimuli acting on nerve ends, rather is it asserted that outer perception, independently of how it takes place, is characterized by onesidedness, non-adequacy, transcendence etc. This is really "intuitive presentation of objects in the flesh" but suffering from certain faults among which only "onesidedness" has been established, but later on the other "faults" come to the fore. But it is not evident that every presentation of cognitive objects in person must have these faults. The sentence in the text says only that in relation to real objects only those which are charged with these "faults" can be perceived directly.

[18] "Deliberate" is here the subset of perceptions belonging to a certain set of them. This set is always limited by the fact that in each perception belonging to it o n e a n d t h e s a m e object is to be given.

[19] I use this word to reproduce the term "gestiftet" which Husserl uses in his later publications beginning with *Formale und Transzendentale Logik*.

This is also what happens to Husserl both in *Ideas I* and in *Lectures on the Phenomenology of Internal Time Consciousness* and later. From this point of view the perceived objects become not only correlates of certain sets of perceptions but, moreover, their creations (or products). More exactly, a reservation is made, it is true, that these are "things perceived as such" or "taken exactly as they are perceived" but, to avoid misunderstanding, it is added that things "in themselves" are spoken of as they are independently of their being perceived. But it is at the same time forbidden in general to speak about such things "in themselves" as something for which experience, if we observe exactly the limits of its validity, gives no justification. Thus, the only thing we "can" justifiably talk about is a "creation" of the relevant cognitive acts.

Thus the fundamental thesis of "transcendental idealism" is obtained: what is real is nothing but a constituted noematic unity (individual) of a special kind of sense which in its being and quality (*Sosein*) results from a set of experiences of a special kind and is quite impossible without them. Entities of this kind exist only for the pure transcendental ego which experiences such a set of perceptions. The existence of what is perceived (of the perceived as such) is nothing "in itself" (*an sich*) but only something "for somebody," for the experiencing ego. "Streichen wir das reine Bewusstsein, so streichen wir die Welt" ("If we exclude pure consciousness then we exclude the world") is the famous thesis of Husserlian transcendental idealism which he was already constantly repeating in lectures during his Göttingen period.

f) In Husserl's work it is possible to find other assertions which, according to him, lead to the same results. This applies mainly to the theory of constitution. Husserl undoubtedly unearthed in this case a certain unusually rich sphere of problems and facts which was hardly known to other investigators. It is possible to indicate only the general outline of these researches and only in so far as they are important for the idealist solution.

Many different constitutive "layers" have to be distinguished in the development of the sets of perceptions of the same thing. After having performed the phenomenological reduction these sets become constant noemas or, as Husserl says, noematic senses

which are to be found at these different layers. These layers are as
it were subordinated or superordinated among themselves and
this order is established through, for example, the fact that to
every noematic sense appearing in a "higher" layer there belongs
an organized set of sense entities belonging to a corresponding
"lower" constitutive layer. This organization springs from the
fact that if the experiencing subject cognizes the elements of a
certain set of noematic senses one after another (crosses it in a
certain sense) then there is "constituted" in them a noematic
sense of the corresponding higher layer which after being constituted appears or, more accurately, offers itself to the subject as
something given. For example: to every perceived thing (after
the reduction: to every thing noema) there belongs a set of
adumbrations through which it appears and is given to the subject. And especially to every intuitively given quality of the
thing there belongs a certain definite set of its adumbrations (or
"profiles," "shades," "perspective views" etc.) which when the
subject cognizes them lead to an intuitive appearance to the
subject of the corresponding quality of the perceived object. A
ball which is uniformly red is given to us when we perceive a
certain set of adjacent shades of red and other colors with varying
degrees of illumination etc., which are continuously interchang-
ing. The rectangularity of the surface of the table at which I am
writing appears in perspective profiles belonging to various points
of view which change constantly, pass one into another when I
e.g. turn my head to the left or to the right or move my head
nearer or further away etc. All this comprises adumbrations of
the same shape, the shape (*Gestalt*) of the table, its rectangularity,
although they differ among themselves and from this shape or, to
be more exact, they all differ with the exception of one series
when I position my eyes at some point or another on a certain
chosen line. They differ in another way when I look only with
the one eye, the left or the right, and in still another way when I
look with both eyes, and so on. These matters are well known
from the theory of perspective. Two moments are, however,
essential here: the adumbrations of a thing are, as I said, perceived (lived) but they are not objectively given phenomena. If
we attended to them as to an object in which we are interested we
could clearly bring the content of a given adumbration to con-

sciousness, but then the corresponding attribute of the thing would cease to be given to us. An adumbration only then carries out the function of presenting this attribute when it is cognized passively and as if in passing (casually) but its function, as it were, increases in strength if the subject cognizes a certain series of adumbrations but not an isolated separate adumbration. The function of presentation consists in the fact that there appears as a concrete datum a certain figure different from the figure appearing in the content of the adumbration: e.g. a rectangle on the basis of a certain rhomboid or trapeze etc., a uniform color of a certain shade on the basis of a spread out, continuous set of many different correspondingly arranged color "blots." This difference of quality given as property of the perceived thing from the one, or better, from the ones which, appearing in adumbrations, show us the quality of the object is the second moment which has to be pointed out here. It is very remarkable and even to a certain extent surprising but, nevertheless, we have to ascertain here the necessary regularity of this order. This general scheme of ordering repeats itself from one constitutive layer to another. For, according to Husserl's assertions, to every adumbration of a certain thing from a certain point of view there belongs a set of noematic sense elements of the corresponding lower constitutive layer in which, in spite of different changes taking place in particular members of this set, the same sense is maintained appearing as constituted in the higher layer, e.g. as content of the same adumbration of this thing. Changes taking place in this deep constitutive layer can be e.g. differences of "sharpness," "expressiveness," saturation, a different degree of blurring going along with different degrees of concentration of attention (attention, note, directed at the thing but not at the adumbrations themselves or their qualitative basis). In spite of these changes in the deep layer of cognized data the same adumbrative *Gestalt* remains an invariant content of a certain adumbration whose function is to determine the *Gestalt* of a thing seen or touched etc. And so on. However these matters are in concrete cases, it is possible to say that in the very final primary basis of our cognition there are sets (or whole poles) of cognized sense-data, orginary, streaming constantly, coming into being in time, losing and acquiring more activity or saturation depending upon

our passive sensitivity or responsiveness. They are placed in the
final primary layer of experiences (doznań) which we in general
realize relatively unclearly, but without this passive experience
we were unable to obtain perceptions of anything although the
experience of it in itself, without any appropriate behavior on the
part of the perceiving subject, is insufficient for the act of perception to take place and for the perception in it of a certain thing
with a corresponding set of intuitively given nature and qualities.
What is the nature of the transition from this final deepest layer
of experiences through ever higher layers to the presentation of
itself as a certain given determined thing in its qualities? How,
on the other hand, does or must the subject behave from the first
experience of final data through a reception of different ordered
changes and qualitative poles until the thing is apprehended in its
qualities? This, in short, is the problem of the so-called constitution of the thing in outer, sense perception.

It is impossible to speak about this here in detail. These matters
have only been investigated to a limited extent and contain great
riches of phenomena and laws of necessary connection among
them. It is sufficient to say that in the far-reaching mutability
of noematic senses of the corresponding lower layer in relation to
the element of the noematic sense of a higher layer this mutability
is not unlimited but, on the contrary, exactly determined. The
passing of the limits entails inevitably the "explosion" of the
sense element constituted on the given basis, in other words: then
this sense element is not constituted and in its place either nothing
appears, i.e. in effect the perception of the particular thing is not
reached or there appears quite another sense of the content of the
adumbration. Taking into account the existence of an ever new
set of the senses of a corresponding lower layer, the sequence of
their experience and also the definite limit of their changeability
and the difference occurring between them as a condition of the
appearance of a certain noematic sense in a constitutively higher
layer, Husserl repeatedly asks the question: what must be contained in the set of noematic senses of a corresponding lower
constitutive layer in order that a certain element of noematic
sense might constitute itself on an immediately higher level?
Husserl tried to solve this problem in different spheres of sense
perception and by noting quite concrete situations. He also

tried to obtain a cross-section of the general scheme of the dependencies arising here and also to determine the general type of the problems which have to be elaborated in this field. This general sense of the problem complex was for Husserl even more important than particular investigations into specific kinds of sense perception. He did not abandon these details for the agenda and was not satisfied by trivial generalizations but tried to elaborate quite concrete cases in order, on their basis, to understand the general sense of the whole set of problems, especially by taking into account the dependence of the constitution of the noematic senses themselves on the behavior and operations of the perceiving subject and, on the other hand, the different behavior or acts of the subject depending on the contents of experience and the appearance there of the noematic senses in a certain order.

When we use the word "dependence" it is clear that what is meant is not only some abstract coordination or subordination of noematic senses and noetic senses but the dependence which can be understood either as a mode of m o t i v a t i n g one kind of senses by others or as the i n v o c a t i o n or t r a n s f o r m a t i o n of noematic senses through the intention of acts and modes of experiencing data by the subject. As I tried to show in another place, as the years passed Husserl tended in his "constitutive" investigations to understand this dependence as a certain kind of a "creation" of noematic sense of a certain layer – in the last resort the noematic sense of a perceived thing – on the basis of the experience of a lower layer by a corresponding behavior by the subject, such or such acts carried out by him or by experiencing the contents of adumbrations or – finally – by acts in which the perception of the thing takes place. As Husserl would agree, this creation is, as a matter of fact, not arbitrarily dependent on the wishes or preferences of the perceiving subject. There is an a p r i o r i lawfulness here which can be disclosed only by a constitutive eidetic inquiry. Husserl dedicated to the solution of this problem decades of work attacking unweariedly ever anew the analysis often of the same situation either to check the results previously gained or under the impact of the awakening of a fresh sensitivity or of the discovery of processes which he had not paid attention to before or had not succeeded in bringing clearly enough to consciousness.

Of course, he did not neglect investigations into changes in the content and mode of carrying out acts of different types on which the mode constituting noematic senses of different layers and types depends. In these investigations was verified the general principle, constantly repeated by Husserl, that to every change in the content and mode of carrying out an act there corresponds an exactly determined change in the corresponding noemas. These noemas turn out to be, if the expression be allowed, "sensitive" to changes occurring in the acts and experiences performed by the subject. Husserl occupied himself particularly with "thetic" acts, i.e. acts consisting in and also containing in their performance certain "theses," acts of positing, asserting the being of something.[20] To the acts which are of many various kinds in their "thetic" character there corresponds in the contents of the corresponding noematic sense a specific existential character, especially the character of "reality," and also e.g. "possibility," "ideal existence" etc. This kind of a character has also its conscious source in the corresponding mode of carrying out the cognitive act, particularly the act of perception. It is, in other words, a certain phenomenon whose sense becomes determined in the mode of carrying out the corresponding cognitive act. "Existence," "reality," "possibility" etc. can be spoken about only after having explained the corresponding acts of pure consciousness but in Husserl's opinion it is not permissible either to speak about the "reality" of something, or, moreover, to claim the reality of a thing or of an object of some kind arbitrarily without appealing to the corresponding acts from which the sense of this reality springs. Not only the very fact of existence but also the sense of its mode "constitutes itself" in a mode essentially necessary in the corresponding acts of pure consciousness. And only in correlation to it is it permissible to speak about it: existence, reality is in its essence something "for" the subject of pure consciousness.

Perceived things, objects of perception that really exist or are only intended, are treated in constitution as being nothing other than elements of a certain specific layer of constituted noematic sense, and whatever is contained in this sense has its constitutive source in the lower noematic layers and ultimately in the experi-

---

[20] Husserl uses here the ambiguous German word "Setzung" or "Setzen" but he speaks also about "Urteilen," about "Doxa," "doxische Momente," "Glaubens-modalitäten" etc.

ences of the primary consciousness and in the relevant noetic acts and is dependent on the above-mentioned factors. It therefore follows that this entire constitutive process yields the ultimate transcendental genesis of things intuitively given to the subject in perception. Thereby the main thesis of transcendental idealism presents itself, that the being of the real world, given to us in an experiential way is dependent on the being and process of the pure constituting consciousness without which it would not exist at all and, secondly, that it is generally awkward even to ask about the existence of the world "in itself" as it transcends the real sense of transcendental constitution whose results create the basis for every inquiry and determine the sense of our questions. The whole world given to us phenomenally in experience (and all the more the world of physics and microphysics construed by thought on the basis of experience) is nothing but a certain definite layer in the process of constitution, a certain phase of "objectification" after which other and further objectifications of a higher order succeed, the results of which are, e.g. the world of microphysics.

Is the whole process of the constitution of the world thereby finally reduced to a primary subjectivity of one Ego or also to a certain open set of constitutive processes taking place in different transcendental subjects remaining in mutual understanding – as occurs e.g. in the scientific cognition of the world but also in daily life when people live together possessing some common interests? Do the positive analyses really reach the most secret depths of primary consciousness or do they stop midway or do they concern only the material determination of the thing or do they discover also the transcendental sources of the thing's categorial structure and the whole plurality called world etc.? These are all just, as Kant would have said, questions concerning the "elegance" of the work and do not concern the theoretical solutions. Basically, nothing essential can be changed if we recognize that every higher element of noematic sense is founded (Husserl says: gestiftet) by the pure Ego in its experience of a plurality of lower noematic senses and in its performance of the corresponding intentional acts or in passive experience; for it is not permissible to distinguish between the "sense" of the thing created in the constitutive process and its existence, between the "phenomenon" of a certain being and its being, between the sense of its existence and the existence itself. No alternative is possible if it is not permissible, and Husserl's point of view entails that it is not, to proceed along the road on which, after having analyzed all the constitutive processes under the sign of phenomenological reduction, this reduction were so to speak cancelled at a certain stage, such that instead of speaking of the sense of existence one could speak, after having clarified this sense, of existence itself, and instead of analyzing the sense of the object one could ask about the object itself, about its essence and its possible existential relation to the perceiving subject or cognition in general. That is, no alternative is possible if it is prohibited (and according to Husserl this prohibition is ensured, as it were, by the senselessness of transcending the transcendental procedure) to stop practicing transcendental phenomenology of the real world at a certain point and begin the search for the metaphysical solution by making use of the results obtained in phenomenology but without tying one's hands with the phenomenological reduction whose application bewitched us into the fairy world of "only the phenomena themselves."

5. THE FORMAL-ONTOLOGICAL FOUNDATIONS OF THE IDEALIST SOLUTION

Undoubtedly, there are several formal-ontological assertions included among the foundations of Husserl's transcendental meditations. They are, however, never distinctly explicated neither in *Ideas* nor in later works although they can be clearly seen in different substantial and decisive conclusions.[21] It is, of course, impossible to delve into all the details of this aspect of the problem. It is, however, necessary to point out certain formal-onto-

---

[21] In order to bring home the formal-ontological basis of different solutions in the controversy between idealism and realism concerning the questions of the existence of the real world I had once to write the whole of the 2nd volume of the *Controversy about the Existence of the World*. Not everything which was set out there plays a role in Husserl's meditations. I also wanted, namely, to explain to myself the formal-ontological basis of other solutions of this controversy. Nevertheless, a good understanding of the Husserlian treatment of the whole problem complex is possible only by taking into account the most important results of my investigations.

logical decisions which played a direct part in Husserl's conversion to the idealist solution.

It begins with two decisions of which one concerns the relation between real objects (taken as they are accessible in outer experience) and the experience of pure consciousness, especially outer perception.

The other is the assertion of a principal difference concerning the essence, on the one hand, of consciousness and, on the other hand, of material (physical) objects. In the first case what is asserted is that the perceived objects, the physical objects, are in their essence transcendent in relation to the experiences of perception in which they are given, this transcendence – as is possible to deduce from the context – consists in there being no part or quality of the object of perception (the thing) as an element or property of the perceptive experience in which it is given. The object and the lived experience (*przezycie*) are in this case two wholes remaining wholly outside each other (for short "transcendent" in relation to each other). The other decision consists in the assertion of a basic difference (emanating from the essence) between physical things and pure consciousness. Spatiality is ascribed to the first though denied to belong to lived experience; and, furthermore, experiences are intentional, but intentionality does not characterize physical things. Conscious experiences and material things are, consequently, not only mutually transcendent but, in addition to that, their essences are different.

To these assertions there is added still another assertion about the relation of the world of real things (may be, of all real things) to the stream of pure consciousness. It seems, in the first analyses, that the stream of consciousness (mine, but likewise other people's consciousness) is in a twofold way related to the real world: a) as the consciousness of real, bodily living essences (istot, Wesen) remaining in causal relations with the environing world of real things, b) by the fact that there is a real relation between the experiences of perception and its subject – according to what psycho-physiology declares on this theme, asserting that perception is causally conditioned by "physical stimuli" acting on nerve ends which in turn evoke such and such perceptive experiences. Thus, consciousness is included in the ensemble of real things and processes and becomes a certain fact appearing inside its limits and dependent in its passing on extraconscious processes. At the same time, Husserl demands that the phenomenological reduction should be carried out and that our natural belief in the existence of the world be suspended. We, ourselves as human beings, come within the scope of the requirements to suspend all belief and, consequently, so too do the facts regarding the individual psyche and consciousness as appearances of natural processes taking place in our body and our soul. At the same time, a certain *residuum* proves to be left which remains outside the framework of the phenomenological reduction and this is, precisely, the pure consciousness of the subject who carries out this reduction. The world along with all living things and their "psychological states" and states of consciousness becomes a certain particular o b j e c t of the acts of pure consciousness whose existence is just "brack-eted." Thus, the pure consciousness seems to be excluded from every relation with the world and the question arises how it could create along with it one whole. Such a whole seems to be created before the reduction as the conscious acts of the philosophizing subject (who is to carry out the phenomenological reduction) seem to belong to the world in a twofold manner. He is connected with it through his acts relating to the objects of the real world and through the processes of his consciousness which is the consciousness of a certain living thing: the man performing the phenomenological reduction. Whereas Husserl declares that no such whole is possible whose elements are both the acts of pure consciousness, on the one hand, and the real objects, particularly the physical, on the other hand. Conscious acts may, in Husserl's opinion, connect themselves in a whole only along with conscious acts, experiences, but cannot create a whole along with material things. In this context Husserl appeals to a certain assertion from formal ontology whose validity just excludes the possibility of connecting experience with things (bodies) in one whole. We read, namely, literally, in *Ideas I*: "Can the unity of a whole be other than one made through the essential proper nature of its parts, which must therefore have some *community of essence* in-stead of a fundamental heterogeneity?"[22] This sentence has the grammatical form of a question but strictly speaking it is a rhetorical question and plays the role of expressing one of the

[22] *Ideen* (1950), p. 88 (1st ed., p. 70). (Eng. transl., p. 126.)

basic assertions of formal ontology. Nor are we surprised when we also read (*loc. cit.*): "A unity determined purely by the proper essence of the experiences themselves can only be the unity of the stream of experience, or, which is the same thing, it is only with experiences that an experience can be bound into one whole of which the essence in its totality envelops these experiences' own essences and is grounded within them."[23] But we know from the statements already quoted that Husserl establishes a fundamental difference between the essence of consciousness and the essence of material things which, according to his personal experience, become the framework of the real world and also of the psycho-physical beings living in it, especially humans.

Thus, thanks to the assumption taken over from formal ontology and the essential difference said to hold between pure consciousness and material (spatial) things, pure consciousness becomes not only excluded from the world (this was asserted already by the phenomenological reduction) but, besides, also excluded from every essential relation to the world, and it cannot create with it a uniform whole. It becomes some kind of a special factor outside the world and opposed to it, and it becomes unintelligible that it can, nevertheless, remain in some relations with it and, moreover, how it can, as the consciousness of certain living beings, remain inside its limits in causal relations with the processes taking place in the world.

The principal difficulties of Cartesian dualism are – as we can see – revived and these difficulties lead with the occasionalists to the exclusion of the possibility of a causal relation occurring between *cogitationes* and *res extensae*, with Spinoza to a psychophysical parallelism between the two attributes of the substance and, finally, with Leibniz to "monads without windows" and the appeal to God for help by establishing the *harmonia praestabilita* between monads.

In any case, this is clear: Either one has to give up any essential unity between pure consciousness and the real world or deny the difference which has its source in their essence or at last understand the relation between the real world somehow quite otherwise and

---

[23] *Ideen* (1950), p. 86 (69). (Eng. transl., p. 125.) Husserl adds to this the observation that this assertion will acquire more clarity and reveal its importance in later investigations.

give up the two factors (existing in the same mode of being and equal in their existence) which could remain between themselves in a real relation of the same type as the members of this unity among themselves. Maybe that the change of the type of relation between them enables us to restore the "unity" between those so heterogenous essences (istności) as pure consciousness and the real material things (the material world, cosmos). Maybe that the change of the type of relation and, at the same time, a changed mode of existence of one of these members will permit us to understand how pure consciousness can "relate itself" to things?

Husserl's answer is clear and univocal: The material things given in perception and thought in the cognitive acts super-structured over perception are not an autonomous (separate in relation to conscious experiences) sphere of autonomous being in itself; they are only something that exists in its essence "for" the conscious subject performing the perceptive acts. They are only intentional units of sense and beyond that *"ein Nichts"* (nothing). As such the unit of a constituted object sense in the process of experience (*doświadczenie, Erfahrung*) is subject to further determinations and modifications in the stream of experiences and this unit belongs of necessity to the corresponding set of conscious acts existing absolutely in the course of their being carried out. In spite of their transcendence in relation to these acts, the transcendence designated by the very intention of the acts, just because they are the creations of a set of conscious acts, they become inevitable correlates of conscious experiences, and their difference of their existence springs from the fact that they are not effective parts of experience[24] but only their intentional creations: "intentional units." In this Husserl sees the principal difference in the mode of existence between consciousness and reality, the most fundamental which – in his opinion – is existing in general.[25] By this emphasis on transcendence of material things in relation to the experiences of perceptions in which they are given, Husserl's idealistic solution is different from other "idealisms" e.g. that of

[24] In German: "reeller Teil des Erlebnisses," especially "reeller Teil der Wahrnehmung" as against "intentionale Einheit," "das identisch-einheitlich Bewusste." Cf. *Ideen I*, p. 91 (73) ff. (Eng. transl., p. 129.)

[25] Cf. *l.c.*, p. 96 (77), (Eng. transl., p. 134): "In so doing we give voice to the most fundamental and pivotal difference between ways of being, that between Consciousness and Reality."

Berkeley. This transcendence is also a certain formal-ontological moment of the situation occurring between the real objects and conscious experiences in which they are given, a moment emanating from, for instance, the formal-ontological assertion about the condition for the unity of the whole of objects, and from the asserted difference between the essence of lived experience and material things. This transcendence enables the recognition of a special mode of existence for what is real[26] as a special mode of existence of things in relation to the mode of existence of consciousness. If what is real was an element of the perceptive experience (e.g. if it were, according to Husserl, a sense datum contained in lived experience) then there could be no difference between it and consciousness in their mode of existence. This mode would be the same as that of conscious acts. This would not be, exactly speaking, an "idealism" but a certain kind of a spiritualistic concept of the real world. The difference between the essence of consciousness and the real, especially the material thing, would be obliterated. This difference is, however, not removed by Husserl, even in the last phase of his investigations when he approached the monadology of Leibniz in his view of the world. On the contrary, he constantly emphasized this difference and arrived, in effect, at his materially and existentially clearly dualistic, transcendental idealism, at least concerning the individual temporally determined being. But taking into account ideal objects whose existence (as intentional) Husserl recognized even in the last phase of his life it can be said that his idealism from the existential-ontological point of view is pluralistic.

[26] This mode of existence was analyzed by me in the *Controversy about the Existence of the World* and I ascribed to it the existential moment of existential heteronomy in contradistinction to existential autonomy which is inherent in the real world's mode of existence.

PART II

CRITICAL REMARKS

Husserl's assertions, presented here, can be inquired into from two different points of view: As assertions in themselves whose truth and theoretical foundations are to be investigated, and, secondly, as arguments which are to prove once and for all Husserl's idealist standpoint in the relation to the real world. I am going to consider them under these two headings.

I. MUST THE CONCEPT OF PHILOSOPHY AS RIGOROUS SCIENCE LEAD TO TRANSCENDENTAL IDEALISM?

The concept of philosophy as rigorous science has a postulatory and programmatic character: Husserl wanted to realize such a philosophy and was convinced that its realization was possible when and only when philosophy became eidetic knowledge about pure consciousness and its intentional correlates obtained in immanent eidetically attuned perception. This postulate can either be accepted or rejected, but its advancement – in itself – seems not to entail an idealistic solution of the problem of the existence of the world. It is possible to doubt the rightness of the premises on which this postulate rests e.g. the assertion about the existence of immanent perception and about its indubitability or correlatively the assertion about the principal dubitability of a direct cognition of the external world. It can also be doubted if philosophy is to obtain "absolute," indubitable knowledge instead of being satisfied with knowledge of the same cognitive value as e.g. the natural sciences are entitled to. Why demand something more from philosophical knowledge? Let us assume, however, that the aspiration to gain as perfect a knowledge as possible is natural and rather common, such that if in the framework of natural sciences we came to the conclusion that we are unable in that framework to obtain this kind of knowledge then it is clearly a surrendering of something that we wished to achieve if only it were possible. If it is the case that we are dissatisfied with scientific knowledge (in the narrow sense of this term) and feel the need for indubitable knowledge and that it can be achieved in immanent perception are not we, then, compelled to take the next step and think that by this immanent perception of cognitive acts we reach the cognition of their objects? These objects, in the case of the real world, are first and foremost the material things given, according to Husserl, directly to the subject carrying out the acts of outer perception, these acts being transcendent in relation to this perception and such that it belongs to their essence that they cannot be given in any other manner but only by carrying out this kind of acts. This means, among other things, that they cannot be given in immanent perception.[1] If, then, rigorous philosophy was to be a phenomenology of pure conscious experiences (acts), performed in immanent perception, then the objects of the real world, especially spatial things (material) would simply have to remain outside the sphere of philosophical investigations. Husserl would certainly also agree to this, asserting that outer perception, as means for acquiring knowledge about material objects (things and processes), is used by representatives of natural science, especially by physicists, chemists and biologists, and that knowledge obtained by them should not, so to speak, be copied in philosophy, particularly not in phenomenology. How can phenomenology, then, assert something about spatial physical things and, particularly, about their mode of existence, their existential relation to pure consciousness, their dependence on the course of perceptive acts etc.? The answer can be sought in two ways. Phenomenologists – particularly at least some representatives of the so-called Göttingen circle of Husserl's pupils and also some of the "Munich" phenomenologists – would answer this question by asserting that,

---

[1] Husserl asserts this clearly: "Thus a basic and essential difference arises between Being as Experience and Being as Thing. In principle it is a property of the regional essence experience (more specifically of the regional subdivision *cogitatio*), that it is perceivable through immanent perception, but it is of the essence of a spatial thing that this is not possible." Cf. *l.c.*, p. 95 (76). (Eng. transl., p. 133.)

certainly, no phenomenologist would like to intrude in the work
of physicists or biologists but, firstly, the natural sciences do not
give answers to various questions concerning these objects, but,
nevertheless, demand answers, e.g. concerning the mode in which
material things exist; and, secondly, when physicists employ
themselves with e.g. individual or general qualities of physical
objects then, first of all, they are interested in the factual
qualities of these objects taken in the fullness of their acci-
dental being and determination whereas phenomenological philosophers are only interested in what kind of essence this kind of
objects has (or would have if they existed effectively) which,
when given in outer perception, are given as physical things
(or processes). In this case, the general essence of this kind of
objects is investigated and, moreover, irrespectively of their
factual existence or whether they only appear to exist and be
such and such. Phenomenologists do not take into account acci-
dental qualities or attributes. There can be cases of a phenomenologist's interest in the essence of certain exactly individual
objects, e.g. of a certain determined person, but that is outside
the framework of the matters which could lead him to be sus-
pected of intruding into the field of physical research. Phenomenologists occupy themselves with the ontology of physical
objects (material things or processes) and suspend their judg-
ment on all matters belonging to the field of research of the
natural sciences. By doing so, they make use of a certain particular mode of outer perception but modified in an essential
manner. Firstly, they neutralize the conviction, inherent in every
such perception, about the real existence of the perceived object
and, secondly, carry them out in the "eidetic" attitude, performing "ideation" on the matter supplied by perception. This
"ideation" in this case is of such a kind that on the basis of a
certain individual matter of perceptive objective data only the
essential and general moments are looked for, i.e. – speaking my
language – the constants of the contents of the general
idea of the material thing. Husserl, on the other hand, trying,
as do the other phenomenologists, to obtain eidetic knowledge of
the objects of knowledge, suggests a slightly different method of
procedure. He is of the opinion that all knowledge of any objects
must be based on correspondingly matched direct cognition and

is the effect of the intentions of cognitive acts contained in them. This is like the consequent use of the postulate of positivism, i.e. to appeal constantly to "experience" with the addition that the concept of "experience" is extended to every direct cognition showing the object in person. Husserl is not satisfied, however, with the analysis – if it can be called that – of ready-made phenomena in which the given objects appear. He demands an eidetic analysis of the very acts entering the field of the acts of direct cognition and the dependency relations between them and in this way controlling the authority of the object sense constituted in the cognitive process determining the nature and qualities of the corresponding objects. Apparently this appeal to conscious acts and the investigation of the whole process of cognition of the given object – in the eidetic attitude – is essentially justified and may eliminate the danger of a certain lack of criticism in a purely ontological research directed straight at the essence of the object of knowledge. But in the practical performance of this task Husserl, not having established sufficiently well in a previous analysis the contents of the sense of the essence of the given object, in the course of his considerations emphasizes too strongly the subjectively directed aspect of his inquiries and, not wanting to perpetrate any dogmatic assertion about the objects of cognition, suddenly adopts the directly opposite point of view, treating the sense of the object constituted in the cognitive process exclusively as the creation of the acts coming into consideration. Consequently, he treats the analyzed objects from the beginning exclusively as intentional correlates of these acts and these objects have only in these acts the source and basis of their existence and such and no other formation of their contents. If this treatment of the sense of objects was only transitory and made possible – after critical investigation of the whole cognitive process – a return to the objects given and the retention of the proper character of their existence, then we were not compelled to an idealistic conclusion – because of the method of investigation. It is not idealism to assert that phenomena, revealing to us certain objects and constituted in certain processes of cognitive acts, are dependent on intentions contained in these acts and in synthetic connections among them and that they are co-conditioned by the existence of these acts. But Husserl, when he

already had gained insight into the process of the constitution of
the object senses (or phenomena) in the course of the corresponding sets of conscious acts, considers this to be a definitive result
and forbids the return to the objects appearing through the
analyzed phenomena, considering the restoration to these objects
of their proper mode of existence to be the "absolutization" of
what – according to him – is existentially relative in relation to
the processes of pure consciousness. Thus, the concept of philosophy as "rigorous" science appealing finally to immanent perception leads Husserl to the conclusion which appears to be in-
compatible with keeping staunchly one's faith to (the application
of) the results of our knowledge to the ultimate data of direct
cognition.

2. THE LIMITS OF THE APPLICABILITY OF THE PHENOMENOLOGICAL REDUCTION

Closely connected to what I said in the preceding section is the
question as to what is the essential function and what are the
limits of applicability of the phenomenological reduction. Husserl
introduces it in *Ideas I* with a clear aim in mind which has nothing
in common, at least not *expressis verbis*, with the correct method
of epistemological investigations. The important matter is the
method of uncovering a separate region of individual being which
is, according to Husserl, pure consciousness. This is the very
region in whose framework the achievement of absolute knowledge is to be possible, an indubitable knowledge obtained in immanent perception or in the "eidetic" attitude to the essence of
the acts of this consciousness. Here there is to take place the
realization of philosophy as "rigorous" science.

But the question how it is possible exclusively on the basis of
pure consciousness to include in philosophical research the whole
of being accessible to the knowing subject by carrying out the
corresponding acts of pure consciousness and if and how it is thus
possible to avoid being committed in advance to the idealist
solution does not belong to the problem of the correct method of
epistemology but to the problem regarding the scope of transcendental phenomenology. Is it to be only eidetic knowledge of pure

consciousness or is it to include also the ontology of different regions of objects which are not this consciousness? This is at the same time the problem concerning the question if the phenomenological reduction, being – at first sight – only a certain methodological operation, is not *de facto* an operation which predetermines in this manner the further course of phenomenological research so that it entails as if automatically a substantial solution of the problem of the existential relation of the world and other regions of being to pure consciousness, whereas as a pure methodical operation it should leave open the possibility of achieving any solution of the problem. The achievement of this solution is to be dependent only on essential facts which can be discovered without any *a priori* bias in the very structure, mode of existence and qualities entering the analysis of objects and whole regions of objects. Does not, then, the phenomenological reduction entail certain fundamentally unclarified foregone conclusions which make impossible purely objective research on the essential facts? Having this role and character as, according to Husserl, means for discovering the region of pure consciousness, the phenomenological reduction does not remain in relation to the problems of the correct method of epistemology. But, nevertheless, it can and does play a role in epistemology other than the role it plays in the introduction to Husserl's transcendental phenomenology; this is precisely because the tasks of epistemology are, in spite of everything, different from those of transcendental phenomenology. "In spite of everything" since in *Ideas I*, especially in Book IV (*Abschnitt*) Husserl treats what are phenomenological problems as problems of epistemology *par excellence*. This leads, perhaps, to a certain unconscious ambiguity of the role of the phenomenological reduction in Husserl's works. In epistemology it is a method for avoiding the error of *petitio principii*, not to mention other possible functions which Husserl ascribes to it. By suspending (in one or another way) the belief in the existence and determination of the objects of knowledge of a certain investigated kind, e.g. of the outer perception, it is to prevent prejudging in a positive manner the cognitive validity of the investigated cognition at the moment when this validity is still to be disclosed or evaluated in the very epistemological investigation (in the so-called "critique" of knowledge). If, e.g., the

critique of the experiential knowledge of physical things is to be
performed, but this critique is obtained in outer sense perception,
then the reduction concerns any possible bias towards the existence and qualification of these things. If, on the other hand, the
question is to disclose and criticize the cognitive value of knowledge concerning other minds (other persons) then the reduction
embraces all prejudice concerning the existence and qualification
of other psychic subjects and their states.[2] When the question is
the problem of the cognitive value of ideal objects (general or
particular ideas or the essence of individual objects) the reduction
must be extended to all prejudices of the existence and qualification of ideas or essences etc. From the application of these
different reductions – which, of course, are not to be carried out
all at once – there emerges a certain problematic concerning an
applied method of epistemological investigations which Husserl
does not elaborate any further.[3] We meet here the principal
difficulty how not to make use, in the investigation on the knowledge of objects of a certain type, of the justified knowledge of
these objects without losing cognitive contact with reality which
concerns the given cognition. In carrying out his research – especially in the IV Book of *Ideas I* called *Vernunft und Wirklichkeit*
(Reason and Reality) – Husserl attempted to use a certain
procedure which culminates in the problems of constitution. I
shall occupy myself later with the method of solving these problems. Now we must consider another matter, namely, what is the
limit of applicability of the phenomenological reduction? Must
all philosophy be carried out on the basis of phenomenological
reductions or is this not necessary? Apparently, the application
of the phenomenological reduction, in one or another form in the
field of the c r i t i q u e of knowledge of one or another kind, is not
only useful but also necessary. Does this, however, entail that all
philosophical research must make some limited use of phenomenological reductions, e.g. in the field of one ontology or another
(e.g. ontology of nature, ontology of the objects of mathematical

---

[2] Husserl does not occupy himself with this problem until his *Cartesian Meditations*.
[3] This is one of the fundamental problems to be solved in *Metodologiczny wstęp do
teorii poznania* (Methodological Introduction to Epistemology) on which I lectured in
the Wrocław Society for the Sciences in 1948 (see the Minutes of this Society for the
year 1948) and which I hope to be able to publish in one of the consecutive volumes of
my *Collected Works*. (Translator's note: This volume was published under the title
U podstaw teorii poznania by PWN, Warsaw 1972.)

research, formal ontology etc.) and also in attempting to solve such metaphysical problems as that of the existence and mode of existence of the real world? This does not seem to me to be necessary. Let us examine this in greater detail.

First of all: If in the theory of knowledge we find ourselves in the field of eidetic analysis of a certain kind of knowledge and the results obtained then, after having carried out the reduction of the knowledge analyzed necessary in this case, we are forbidden to make any assertions about the objects of the knowledge investigated either in the course of the investigation or in the form of assumed or suppressed premises (as e.g. about physical stimuli acting on nerve ends in our sense organs). We are not permitted in the course of these investigations to assert that material things are "nothing else" than intentional entities of the sense constituted in a certain set of acts, nor that they in one or another way are in their being dependent on pure consciousness. In the field of epistemological investigations it is only permitted to say about them how they are meant in the corresponding cognitive acts, how they would have to exist if they existed at all and were such as they are meant to be. Only when the critique of the corresponding cognition is completed, and we know what cognitive value we are entitled to ascribe to the results acquired in it, are we justified in asserting something about these objects on the basis of the critical knowledge obtained about their cognition. They were a certain kind of ontic (or, if you like, metaphysical) consequences from the results of epistemological analyses. They would no more belong to epistemology but to ontology or metaphysics appealing to the results of the first theory. The phenomenological reduction would not be binding on these results and there would be neither justification nor point in applying it. This is so if we agree that epistemology does not exhaust the problems of every philosophical investigation, i.e. that no philosophical research is allowed outside the theory of knowledge. There were several cases where attempts were made to limit philosophy to epistemological research—especially from the time of a one-sided interpretation of the results gained in Kant's *Critique of Pure Reason*. But we must accept one of the following alternatives: Either (1) that philosophical research has to be limited to epistemological investigations – and, at that, as some want, to limited descriptive analysis of the cognitive processes without trying to perform a critique of the cognitive value of the results obtained in one or another cognition. But in this case the solution of the controversy between idealism and realism in relation to the real world and particularly the very solution according to transcendental idealism is quite impossible to reach and we have to resign from any assertions about the existence and qualifications of the world, especially from those which are veiled behind various epistemological concepts and conclusions. – Or (2) that it is not justifiable to limit philosophical research to epistemology, and in this case assertions about the real world – either in the form of metaphysical assertions ascribing to this one world taken *in individuo* this or that character of existence etc., or in the form of eidetic assertions pronouncing this or that on the essence of this world (on its possible mode of existence and on its nature) – would have to be free from the obligation to apply the phenomenological reduction, and either from the one which neutralizes our empirical forejudging about the existence and qualifications of the world or from the other which would also neutralize the corresponding thetic moments of the cognition of the idea of reality or the idea of material things etc. This does not exclude, of course, that the result, which we would then obtain was itself an idealist solution. But it would not be smuggled into the field of epistemological investigations but would either be a simple conclusion of critical-epistemological research applied to knowledge of the world acquired by us factually or it would also be independent of epistemology and would only be the result of separately organized research on the ontology of the real world or also of an independently organized metaphysics of the real world. Whether it is and to what extent it is possible does not belong to our theme here. For us the only important thing is that the idealist solution cannot appear as a simple entailment of the use of the phenomenological reduction when it is limited to epistemological research and, what is more, at its very beginning when the task is to gain the region of the cognitive acts of pure consciousness. I agree that in a certain phase of epistemological investigations it is useful to perform them – so to speak – on the basis of pure consciousness but not on the basis of a psychophysiology of human cognition taking place in the real world.

I agree that the discovery of pure consciousness (without further metaphysical premises) is needed and indispensable although this cannot be justified here.[4] But this reduction is not to lead, as it does in Husserl's *Ideas I*, to propositions about real objects neither in the spirit of the "realist" nor of the "idealist" solution.[5] If this is done by Husserl then it is a violation of the right method of epistemology. Even the very discovery of the region of pure consciousness must be performed in such a way that by using the phenomenological reduction it is unnecessary to appeal, e.g., to the difference in the mode of existence of what is real and what is pure *cogitatio*. And in this matter – as far as Husserl in fact appeals to this difference of mode of existence – a corresponding reservation has to be made.

3. CRITICAL REMARKS ON PARTICULAR RESULTS OF THE ANALYSIS OF OUTER PERCEPTION AND THE THEORY OF CONSTITUTION

a) The transcendence of real objects in relation to the acts of direct cognition, particularly to acts of outer perception.

One must agree with Husserl's assertion that perceived physical things, taken exactly as they are perceived, are "transcendent" in relation to the acts of outer perception (the "transcendent" one). But it has to be taken into account in what sense exactly we may understand this proposition if we want to hold it in the field of eidetic phenomenology, i.e. of investigations based on the phenomenological reduction. Husserl, as a matter of fact, introduces them as a certain kind of initial proposition prior to the introduction of the reduction itself (whose sense and function he announced earlier but whose execution is to be effected later, the introductory examination being aimed at convincing us that it is possible to perform it without losing the possibility of arriving at statements about the objects of the cognitive acts of pure consciousness) but it is to be valid also when we have carried this

---

[4] This is one of the themes investigated in *Metodologiczny wstęp do teorii poznania* which I mentioned above.

[5] I add quotation marks as both terms are equivocal and it is impossible to analyze here the different meanings they have had in the history of European philosophy.

reduction out and occupy ourselves anew with the analysis of outer perception.

Is it also possible to understand these investigations as a metaphysical proposition or simply as an empirical one about physical things? This is not the case as Husserl clearly states that he affirms something which belongs to the essence, on the one hand, of the experience of pure consciousness called outer (sense) perception, and, on the other hand, to the essence of physical, spatial things. In more exact terms (but not exactly in the Husserlian formulation)[6] it belongs to the general idea of something such as a material, physical thing that it cannot be an effective part (echter Teil) of the perceptive experience or any experience in general and must, accordingly, be perceivable only in outer perception but never in immanent perception. This leads to a different manner in which something is given through "adumbrations" (Abschattungen) or, more accurately, presented in sets of adumbrations which cannot be applied to any experiences of pure consciousness given in immanent perception to the subject who experiences them.

The Husserlian statement under discussion has to be accepted, in my opinion. But his propositions about objects, such as material objects, go much further than I am willing to go. On this basis Husserl 1) speaks about two modes of existence: Being as reality (Sein als Realität) and being as experience (Sein als Erlebnis), 2) instead of limiting himself to the proposition on the essence (idea) of material things he proclaims this proposition and extends it to anything which is real and 3) states that "the spatial thing" (Raumding) is nothing but intentional entity which can be in principle given only as unity of this kind of modes of appearance[7], i.e. through "adumbrations."

---

[6] Husserl uses the words "essence" and "idea" of something (Wesen and Idee) interchangeably. He distinguishes "Wesen in der Konkretion" from "Wesen" in general, that is essence concretized in a certain individual object which is its essence from "essence" taken idealiter, but he did not analyze any further the difference between them, that is, between "essence," incarnated in some object, and ideas, whether they be general or particular. After Jean Hering took the first step in the analysis of these matters I proceeded further in my Essentiale Fragen (1925). In spite of that, it is permissible in the given case to use the expression – idea of a material thing – as I am speaking about Husserl's theories in Ideas I.

[7] "On the other hand, a spatial thing is no other than an intentional unity, which, in principle, can be given only as the unity of such ways of appearing." L.c., p. 98 (78). (Eng. transl., p. 135.)

It has to be emphasized that in the text of *Ideas I* preceding these assertions there are no analyses which would show that everything real, and not only material things, must in its essence (general idea) be perceivable exclusively in transcendent (outer) perception. But there is a statement which could serve Husserl as a justification for making this generalization. We read namely: *"Denn leicht überzeugt man sich, dass die materielle Welt nicht ein beliebiges Stück, sondern die Fundamentalschicht der natürlichen Welt ist, auf die alles andere reale Sein wesentlich bezogen ist."*[8] If everything real, – but in this quotation Husserl undoubtedly means psycho-physical selves of other people, particularly the psychic life and qualities of character of the persons with whom we live, – has as its basis the layer (stratum) of material bodies then, e.g., the psychic facts of other people are accessible to us at least through the outer perception of others' bodies (*Leib*) and they are, consequently, transcendent in relation to these perceptions although they themselves are not spatial but only founded in what is spatial (bodily).

However, even if we agree with Husserl that he is justified in moving from the explication of the transcendence of spatial things to the transcendence of everything real,[9] it is nevertheless legitimate to doubt whether by simply pointing out the difference between the spatial thing and the experience in pure consciousness resulting from the opposition between the transcendence of the one and the immanence of the other with regard to direct perception is sufficient to justify ascribing to things a different mode of existence from that of experience, and so different that Husserl sees in it *"die prinzipielle Unterschiedenheit der Seinswei-*

---

[8] "For it is easy to convince oneself that the material world is not just any portion of the natural world, but its fundamental stratum to which all other real being is essentially related." *L.c.*, p. 87 (70). (Eng. transl., p. 126.) It is surprising to read that "it is easy to convince oneself" about this, as it is *de facto* possible to think that here is hidden one of the most difficult problems of the structure of our real world. Agreement is made more difficult by Husserl's speaking here about the "natural" world, i.e. a world understood as it is approached in the "natural" attitude we take in everyday life and it is unclear if and to what extent we are permitted to consider this "natural" world as "real" *sensu stricto*.

[9] In this case it has to be recognized that our own experiences as our own psychic facts as psycho-physical individuals (people) are transcendent in relation to "inner" perception, as they have to be called, in distinction from immanent perception. This is in my opinion, justified, especially concerning perception or any mode of direct knowledge (if it exists!) or the attributes of our own character or the so-called soul; but Husserl nowhere spoke out clearly on this theme. Husserl's volume called *Phänomenologische Psychologie* is now in print. These matters may be treated there.

sen, die kardinalste, die es überhaupt gibt, die zwischen Bewusstsein und Realität."[10] Is the reason for this kind of difference the fact that something is an "effective part" of an experience or not? Husserl does not make clear those modes of existence which are here in question. We must discover this for ourselves by inference from other things he says. I shall return to this. Now, it must be noted that belonging or not belonging to a certain stream of experiences and thereby to a certain Ego could become the basis for claiming that a different mode of existence is involved only if the same Ego, or its stream of consciousness in its essence, existed otherwise than everything which does not belong to it as an effective part. But then this particular essence of the Ego or of conscious experiences has to be shown and independently of the matter of immanence or transcendence. As can be seen from other results he obtains, which I shall look at later, Husserl also takes this view but it is not clear whether he always fulfills the above-mentioned precondition for a valid demonstration that the Ego and its pure consciousness enjoy a special mode of existence.

In any case, it has to be asserted that from the very fact of the transcendence of material things in relation to outer perception, in which they are given, there does not follow the proposition concluding Husserl's investigation of the transcendence of spatial things which I mentioned under 3 on page 44. Why should something, which appears in a definite set of adumbrations (*Abschattungen*) and which can be given only in that way be "only an intentional entity" and – as Husserl more than once adds – "nothing more"? Why could it not through retaining that form be something existing in itself and independently of individually performed perception? Does it not just belong to the essence of something such as "a spatial thing" that it cannot be given in perception except through adumbrations and does not this postulate that this kind of a thing must be such in itself that it could be given in a set of transcendent perceptions and cannot be given immanently? If it were only an intentional entity and not "really" spatial then there would be no such necessity, for then everything, so to speak, would depend on the lived experience itself and on the mode in which it designates the intentional

---

[10] Cf. *l.c.*, p. 96 (77), (Eng. transl., p. 134): "the most fundamental and pivotal difference between ways of being, that between Consciousness and Reality."

entity belonging to it. The idealist thesis applied to spatial material things does not then follow neither from the fact of transcendence nor from the fact of the appearance of things through "adumbrations."

An attempt could, of course, be made to formulate Husserl's proposition in another way by saying that this "only" does not concern the "intentional unity" in itself but simply the fact that it appears only in just such "adumbrations" or "shades," as Husserl describes them, and cannot appear in any other sets of adumbrations. This would, maybe, suggest a doubt if this is an essential necessity springing from the essence of the spatial thing, if these adumbrations could be otherwise or maybe quite otherwise, if the form which is known to us men (and does not apply to an X-ray exposure) is not conditioned to the same extent by the properties of the perceiving subject. But these matters are not directly connected with the idealism-realism problem and I am not going to elaborate them any further.

b) The onesidedness and inadequacy of outer perception and the consequences following from this.

From the fact that in outer perception material things are always given "from one side" and inadequately and that neither one nor the other can be eliminated even in the infinite process of perceiving there follows only that in no finite process of perception of a certain thing can we be certain that it really exists and is such as it is perceived or was perceived prior to a certain moment. This is not the case in the case of immanently perceived conscious experience. And, in consequence of this, Husserl, quite justly, writes in the title of sect. 46 of *Ideas I*: "*Zweifellosigkeit der immanenten, Zweifelhaftigkeit der transzendenten Wahrnehmung.*" ("Indubitability of Immanent, Dubitability of Transcendent Perception.") This is, however, to go no further than Descartes, although the Husserlian motivation – by appealing to the essential structure of both types of perception and not only to the occurrence of illusions in the field of outer perception as Descartes does – is incomparably deeper. This proposition in itself does not entail, however, any essential difference in the very mode of existence of what is given in these perceptions. It does not justify the proposition contained in the title of sect. 44 where we read: "*Bloss phänomenales Sein des Transzendenten, absolutes*

Sein des Immanenten." ("The merely phenomenal being of the transcendent, the absolute being of the immanent.") Neither does it justify what we read in sect. 55: *"Alle Realität seiend durch Sinngebung."* ("All reality exists through the dispensing of meaning.") In the text of this section we read: *"Alle realen Einheiten sind 'Einheiten des Sinnes'"* and *"Sinneseinheiten setzen ... sinngebendes Bewusstsein voraus, das seinerseits absolut und nicht selbst wieder durch Sinngebung ist." "Eine absolute Realität gilt genau so viel wie rundes Viereck. Realität und Welt sind hier eben Titel für gewisse gültige Sinneseinheiten ...."*[11] It cannot be doubted that it can be said about synthetic intentions, even if they are fulfilled with intuitive data, that they are entities of sense and that these entities (unities) are designated by corresponding perceptions remaining in connection with them and "nothing more," but to say about them that they are i d e n t i c a l l y t h e s a m e as things or other kinds of objects appearing in these sense unities and that these things are, therefore, something "phenomenal," that they exist only by "giving sense in correspondingly assorted acts of consciousness" seems to be quite unjustified – if it is not supported by further arguments. Moreover, if to refer to such unities of sense, existing through "giving sense" but not to material things, is to refer to the fact that transcendent perceptions are "dubitable," if it is to be valid about them that their very existence is not certain but only probable on the basis of a vast collection of unison experience, then one has to protest according to Husserl's own opinions. The very "unities of sense," obtaining their contents and their (purely phenomenal) "existence" from the acts of perceptions giving them sense, a r e n o t a n d c a n n o t b e d o u b t e d i n t h e i r e x i s - t e n c e whereas the source of their existence is just in the very meaning-giving acts, i.e. in transcendent perceptions, and they are the inevitable effect of these acts. Perceptions are not dubitable in relation to them, nor could they exist or be otherwise than they seem to be just on the basis of perceptive acts and on

---

[11] "All real unities are 'unities of meaning'." "Unities of meaning presuppose ... a sense-giving consciousness, which, on its side, is absolute and not dependent in its turn on sense bestowed on it from another source." "An absolute reality is just as valid as a round square. Reality and world, here used, are just the titles for certain valid unities of meaning ...." *Ideen I*, p. 134 (106). (Eng. transl., p. 168.)

the basis of intuitive sense unities. "Unities of sense" must be exactly such as the sense which is "given to"them by perceptive acts; not in relation to them are perceptions "onesided" or inadequate, only in relation to something which itself – if it exists – is independent of perceptive acts and goes beyond the data of onesided perceptions, something which is or is not, not deriving its existence from the "meaning-giving" sets of performed acts of perception. In other words, when Husserl appeals to the fact that outer perception only from a certain point of view, from a certain side always and in its essence apprehends material things, or in general the real, then he has in mind something which is not barely "sense unity" that either can or cannot exist by conservation (or in the worst case only modification) of acts of pure consciousness by whose performance it is directly given, maybe, just because it does not derive its existence from "meaning-giving" but is autonomous in relation to it and in its existence. In other words, from the thesis of the onesidedness and eventual inadequacy of outer perception not only does the purely phenomenal mode of existence of real things not follow but on the contrary this thesis has only meaning and seems only to be justified when we oppose reality, independent in its being from the correspondent acts of consciousness to these unities of sense which acquire the given sense from acts of perception. And only then does it seem to be correct to say that real things are given in a different way – through *Abschattungen* – from the acts of perception themselves and even all the "unities of sense," assuming we retain the distinction between things and unities of sense on the grounds that these unities are not given through *Abschattungen* although they are constituted on their basis as something transcending their contents and although they are perhaps not given in the same way as the conscious acts themselves. But that is a matter which I shall not be concerned with any further. In any case, however, the distinction between "unities of sense" and real things appearing through them or in them makes it possible to agree that the mode in which things are given is different from the mode in which pure experiences are given or may be given. This distinction is what makes up an opposition to transcendental idealism. Transcendental idealism should not appeal to the onesidedness and inadequacy of outer perception and to a different mode of givenness of material things in relation to the mode in which conscious experiences are given.

c) Further arguments in favor of idealism appeal to the fact that in no finite perceptive process of experience can we get certainty as to what is really the nature and qualities of the perceived object itself (thing or process) as it is not known whether the nature, under whose aspect we perceive it, is merely a synthetic aspect defined by previous experience, an aspect which can be modified or entirely dissolved by consequent experience. Because of this there is no basis any longer for distinguishing between a particular thing as it is in itself and this synthetic aspect, the intuitively given "sense" of the object; it is never possible to transcend this sense which is relative and dependent on previous experience. The claim that the given thing has its own nature cannot be verified in the course of experience. It has, therefore, to be abandoned and the view adopted that there is no basis for recognizing objects "in themselves" and everything which we contact in perception exists only "for" the knowing subject, it is only the intentional correlate of sets of perceptive acts belonging to it.

Is this decision justified? We must first of all make it clear that if it was really justified then some deceptions would emerge in the course of perceptive experience of one and the same object. Because in every genuine outer perception[12] the object given in it bears the intuitive character of something "in itself" or something that is in itself and presents itself to us in perception in its proper nature and qualities but not as something which is nothing in itself and is only a "phenomenon" for us. According to the argument quoted we would have to give up this character of being something in itself, of being in itself something different from the perceiving subject. We would then find this something in our real environment. It would not be created by us – as it would have to be if the object were identical with the intuitive sense created in the course of experience. To the contents of this sense belongs, for instance, the existential character of the object

---

[12] That is, those that can be distinguished from hallucination; and perceptions in which illusions occur are revealed as illusions in the course of experience by another controlling experience and eliminated from the set of perceptions whose results are recognized as authentic knowledge of the object.

appearing through adumbrations – the character of something not created by us but only found.

Somebody might say: too bad! – There is such a deception in our perceptive cognition of material things. Consequently, a fiction about something which exists in itself; a fiction which we are never, strictly speaking, properly justified to accept remains imaginary and unverifiable. Reference by idealists, and Husserl is one of them, to things as being given in every perception in person[13] does not dissolve this delusion. Because, as the course of experience with the help of ever more exact modes of perception shows – with the help of devices like the magnifying glass, the electronic microscope etc. – and as, in addition, certain observations compel us to accept different situations created by experiments (as e.g. lines of interference on a screen) etc. – this givenness of things in person does not guarantee to us at all that they exist in the manner in which they appear to us merely in a certain selected string of perceptions. Furthermore, we are at a certain moment forced not only to deny that they have the qualities clearly given us in perception – as e.g. colors, smoothness and even shape – and even agree that where one particular thing is given, e.g. a piece of metal or wood, not to mention such things as, e.g. the table at which I am writing or my own body, there exist many other objects very different as e.g. molecules, cells, atoms etc. The very course of experience compels us to question that things are given to us in their own nature such as they are but this is only an appearance which cannot be verified. We have to agree that if things are given in perception as this or that and thus or thus then they are so only for us and only in a certain phase of the performed perceptive experience. And it is not otherwise when we take into account the qualification and nature of what we have to agree in the course of experience as existing instead of them (physical and chemical objects etc.) as they (when they are no longer given to us directly but only intended on the basis of the process of experience) are such only for us men

---

[13] Some are of the opinion that only a representative concept of outer perception leads to an idealist solution, and that presentationism in the understanding of this perception guarantees us a "realist" solution. Husserl's research on perception shows that this is far from so; that declaring, as Husserl and other phenomenologists do, that in outer perception things are given in person ("sind in ihrem leibhaften Selbst gegeben" – as Husserl says) can, nevertheless, lead to an idealist solution.

having at our disposal such or such experiences. They obtain, then, other qualifications and another nature as soon as new facts emerge in experience (e.g. a change in the explanations of the nature of light in the physical sense after the establishment of Compton's effect or the change in the explanation of the structure of atoms after the explosion of the atom or as the effect of research on cosmic rays). Their intended qualities are only – so to speak – "assorted" to the hitherto obtained results of experience and thought operations aimed at maintaining a unified view of the real world, but are not the qualities or nature of something in itself. The changeability in the history of the development of natural science of the mode of understanding the micro-world shows best of all – according to the view of the defenders of the idealist solution and Husserl himself was of a similar opinion[14] – that we have here only a further phase of the process of objectification in the course of experience and an intuitive sense (or in a merely intentional one) co-ordinated with the given phase, of what "exists" and that means "is for us such or such."[15]

In spite of a strong tendency among theoretical physicists nowadays to recognize the idealist interpretation of different theories concerning situations discovered in the framework of microphysics it is not yet, in my opinion, an established truth that the facts referred to are a sufficient basis for adhering to the idealist solution in the controversy between idealism and realism. We have to recognize that in the framework of exclusively phenomenologically conducted epistemological investigations we

[14] In the works of Husserl with which I am familiar only in *Ideas I* are there certain undoubtedly introductory investigations on the theme of physical objects but there is no systematically laid-out phenomenological theory of physical cognition up to and including the microphysics of the 20th century. But comments in sect. 40 and 52 are not conclusive and were, it must be noted, written before contemporary physics came into being.

[15] Cf. *l.c.*, p. 127 (100), Eng. transl., p. 161): "It is clear from the foregoing that even the higher transcendence of the physical thing does not imply any reaching out beyond the world for consciousness, or, shall we say, for any Ego that functions as the subject of knowledge (singly or in the relation of empathy)." Page 128 (101), (Eng. transl., p. 162): "Thus the implied absurdity, that of turning physical nature, this intentional correlate of logically determining thought, into an absolute, passes unnoticed." Page 129 (102), (Eng. transl., p. 163–164): "We now see clearly at any rate, and our own purposes require this, that the transcendence of an existent (Seins) which constitutes itself within consciousness and remains fettered to consciousness, and the regard we pay to the mathematically grounded science of Nature (whatever the special enigmas may be to which its knowledge gives rise) does not affect our results in the least."

have no possibility of confronting synthetically obtained results concerning the nature and the qualities of things and processes given to us in perception with, so to speak, reality itself as it is in itself, so reaching a solution to the question what is the perceived things' own nature and what is the cognitive value of results arrived at in experience. But exactly the fundamental idea of the constitutive analysis itself and, particularly, that of what Husserl calls *"eine Rechtsbetrachtung"* is based on the determination of the truth and objectivity of cognitive results obtained in direct perception and in the thought operations built on it without referring to this unrealizable confrontation of "reality itself" with the cognitive results. Only, if the expression be allowed, 'at the end" of this investigation and at least after having reached some decisive results is it permissible to draw such conclusions regarding perceived things or physical objects as those which I discussed. But these theses appear at the very beginning of the unrolling of the problems of the so-called transcendental phenomenology. It depends upon the process of this "constitutive problem set" how we are to behave towards the asserted – in my view indubitable – facts that the nature of the perceived thing is the form in which it is intuited intentionally and virtually its intuitive sense is synthetically produced in the course of a set of experiences concerning the given object and of logical operations applied to the previous experience, and it cannot be decided in advance that the perceived thing itself and its nature or qualities is "pure intentional correlate"and "nothing more." Everything depends upon our ability to construe a method of investigation such that it would permit us to solve the problem of justification of this and not another creation of intuitive sense of the given thing and its nature. One of the main guidelines of these investigations must be the principle – which seems to be evident – that in the cognitive process those and only those results are recognized as "knowledge" or as "truth" which in their sense ascribed to a certain reality must be adjusted to this reality itself both concerning its character of existence and its form and also its nature and qualities. This adjustment can be reached if the results obtained in the cognitive process do not contain in themselves moments whose appearance in them were drawn exclusively from creative operations or modes of behavior of the knowing subject, independent of the object of research, which would add something or transform it in its own way derived from the activity and qualities of the subject but would not be only to uncover what is given in experience and an operation of understanding both of these data and the different conditions in which they appear. It is necessary in this matter that the decision on which of our cognitive operations are "creative" and which only "reproductive" and emanating from the adaptation to data be taken not on the basis of unverifiable premises or hypotheses about human nature, about the object of knowledge, or about stimuli acting on the so-called senses, but that it be reached exclusively in analysis, performed in immanence, of the knowing subject's conscious (particularly of cognitively conscious) behavior and operations. The "creative" character or, on the other hand, the character of "the reproductive adjustment and understanding of data" is to be disclosed in such an analysis of consciousness and in investigations concerning the functions of particular operations and behavior of the conscious subject and their role in obtaining cognitively justified results enlightened by "constitutive" analysis. In spite of changes taking place in our conception of the nature of material things it is far from evident that these changes will go on *ad infinitum* and that we will never reach a disclosure of such a nature and such a determination of material things that prove to belong definitively to the things themselves in their own being. This is, however, Husserl's thesis and this made it impossible to contrast the changeable (in the course of experiential cognition) synthetic sense of the nature of what is material and real and its nature. But the impossibility of this contrast must not be interpreted in the sense of the idealist solution because it could as well be interpreted in the sense of the sceptical thesis of unknowability of the nature of material (or in general: real) things. No finite experience or the analysis of it justifies our taking such a decision.

Undoubtedly, Husserl made many attempts to carry out a constitutive investigation. We shall now see whether his positions thus acquired compel us to accept his idealist thesis or if there are some doubts about its legitimacy in spite of his important results.

d) There is no justification for appealing to the fact that from the whole theoretically infinite set of possible perceptions of a certain thing only a finite quantity can become actualized as an argument for the thesis that we do not have the right on the basis of these perceptions to assert anything about this thing itself and that we can only treat it as an intentional correlate of already actualized perceptions. The fact referred to – indubitable in itself – gives us only the right to assert that our knowledge about the given thing acquired in the stated way is not absolutely certain, i.e. it is not excluded that the given thing either does not exist in spite of all the evidence of prior experience or that it is of another nature or otherwise qualified than it should be according to the data of previous experience. The question whether somehow it is possible to obtain such an absolute certainty, i.e. exclude this principal possibility of being otherwise than hitherto acquired experience says, is a special problem. Maybe there is up till now no known method of solving it. The problem itself is not absurd – as idealists claim at times – any more than the character of the existence of the perceived thing is to depend upon the solution of this problem: whether the thing is something in itself or an "intentional correlate" of a set of perceptions and "nothing more." The problem is not absurd as its formulation is delimited by the essential and factual contents of the sense of the very perceptions of every thing. It belongs to this content that a thing which we perceive is given to us – appears – in a certain definite character of its mode of existence: it is given as something which we find as existing without relation to our perceiving it or not, which is what it is although we do not perceive it and what through our perception – in itself – cannot be violated in any way neither in its existence nor in its qualities: it is given as transcendent as remaining outside perception as something in relation to which perception is powerless because it does not exist and is something thanks to perception. Things are given to us in that way. If in some (illusory) perception, or better in some cycle of perceptions, it appears that what is intuitively given reveals itself as dependent on the mode of perception or its conditions, in a certain aspect imposed on the object by perception or another behavior of the subject, then this series of perceptions becomes excluded from the set of perceptions which supply us with knowledge about the given object. And this exclusion occurs – so to speak – by itself in the framework of the cognitive process itself without any need of referring to the deliberations of the epistemologist discussing the particulars of the cognitive process and somehow evaluating their role in the acquisition of the critically examined cognitive result. The particular perceptions in their motivative functions are capable of confirming or weakening the results obtained in other perceptions of the same thing or a whole objective situation in which it (the thing) participates and this confirmation or weakening consists in the fact that the results subjected to the doubt (weakening) delivered by some perception or a cycle of perceptions come to be regarded as not corresponding to the thing itself, as false or illusory. The very experience determines the sense in which the things given in it are to exist and that is the very sense, or mode of existence, autonomous in relation to experiences (i.e. self-existing and independent of experiences founded in immanence of the determination of the given thing in itself). It is not true, then, that the perceptions of a certain thing obtained up to the given moment present it to us as existing "for us" only as an exclusively intentional unity of sense and that, therefore, we are obliged to ascribe to things just such a mode of (intentional) being and no other, neither is it true that ascribing to them an autonomous being is transgressing the limits of competence bestowed upon us by previous experience. Just by not committing this transgression and by keeping strictly to the information supplied to us by previous perceptions selected by motivative connections between perceptions we have the right and duty to ascribe to perceived things or other objects recognized by the cognitive subject on the basis of experience the character of autonomous being; and this does not exclude the possibility that the certainty of this ascription is limited or supplied with reservation that it may in principle happen that the information supplied to us about the given thing is false, i.e. – in the limiting case – that a thing with such a nature and such qualities about which the given object-sense informs us, does not in fact exist. But – and this seems to be decisive – even if it happened (as happened to us more than once) that we really reached such a conviction, it does not follow at all that a thing about whose existence we were convinced in the course of experience is *de facto* "purely intentional correlate" of a certain set of cognitive acts, but that it does not exist in general, viz. in the sense of autonomous existence. But if there exists intentionally at the same time this perceptive s e n s e or – taken more generally – the sense of some cognitive act of thought, then its existence cannot, so to speak, replace the existence of the given thing autonomously non-existing, neither can it in any way change the fact of its non-existence. In particular this situation cannot transform the proper sense of the mode of existence of the real physical things (as far as they exist at all) into purely intentional existence.

If this is to be generalized for all objects of outer experience, i.e. if it were possible to show that all object-senses (*sensy przedmiotowe*) misinform about certain real objects[16] then it has only to be said that such a world which would correspond exactly to these misleading senses does not exist, not that the real world so determined is indeed only the purely intentional correlate of the whole ensemble of experience. This other "world" can never be made primary and the first cannot be made secondary; between them there is a vital difference in mode of existence. The second, purely intentional correlate of the whole of experience, can indeed seem or masquerade as the first; but if there are cognitive reasons for showing that it is only an appearance of being something which it is not in fact then this does not obliterate the difference between them but highlights it. There are no grounds then for accepting the idealist point of view. Either the agnostic position in relation to the real world is possible or the position recognizing that the real world does not exist at all. But if there is no reason for the view that all object-senses obtained in experience are misinformative about the world, then there is no ground for r e j e c t i n g the realist concept of the world, although it is insufficient for a s u b s t a n t i a t e d a c c e p t a n c e of this conception. But this is a matter which cannot be examined more closely here.

---

[16] So far such a limiting situation is unknown. Always, so far, when it happened that a certain thing which we considered as existing did not really exist then this non-existence was, if it can be so put, only an exclusion from a certain region of being of the world, non-existence in the limits of this region which at the same time is considered as existing. It can also justly be asked whether the realization of the limiting case put forward here is in general possible in principle.

e) It is certain that the perceptions, connected together by motivative bonds, of one and the same thing lead to the "constitution," as Husserl says, of a certain more or less unified intuitive sense of this object, that this sense is a particular product of the whole cognitive process. But it does not follow at all that the object in this sense is also its synthetic product and a product, moreover, if it can be so put, exclusively created by the cognitive (perceiving) subject. By "exclusively," as applied to the sense, is meant that on its creation, with precisely such a content as it happens to have in a certain definite case, nothing has an influence which did not have the source of its existence in the very perceiving subject, or where phenomenal "data" were not designated by this subject or an activity of the subject, e.g. synthesization of results, their interpretation etc. The subject's decision to carry out this activity would be totally arbitrary and its performance as well. And it would be co-designated by nothing different from it. It has to be added that this production of such an object-sense would unavoidably lead to the existence of the corresponding object or else it would not be permissible to differentiate between the intuitive sense of a certain object (or, if you like, a certain purely intentional object) and an object existing autonomously and having exactly such qualities which this sense gives it. It seems, in spite of all the suggestions put forward by Husserl, that it is impossible to agree to any of these points.

Let us begin by examining if the "sense" of an object perceived in a certain finite set of uniform perceptions can be "exclusively" – in the given sense – created by the perceiving subject. The root of the matter is evidently in the question of the existential character and the source of existence of the so-called sense data. Already G. Berkeley had difficulties with them and had to refer to the actions of God in order to explain the so-called resistance of what he called "impressions" to the attempts of the subject (*spirit*) to get rid of these impressions or bring about changes in them. After that only German idealists in the style of Fichte tried to deduce them from the Ego as the first Non-Ego but these attempts are not convincing. The subject cognizing sense data feels them as something alien to him and rather, as it were, invading him and he tries at least to grasp them by receiving them (making them clear to himself); but if they are, for one reason or another, disagreeable, then he tries to evade cognizing them but not by a simple *sic jubeo* of his conscious act – because that would be too weak – but by appropriately chosen bodily actions (which appear in correspondingly chosen "impressions" of muscles and joints). Purely conscious behavior of the subject towards the cognized sense data can modify them to a certain extent, e.g. by turning the attention to or from them, by "objectifying" them etc. – but this does not alter the fact of their "otherness" and their at least relative independence of the cognitive subject. This leads the subject to the conclusion that sense data are not the product of his own conscious acts but something which has its source of existence outside the cognitive subject although it can be in its various details co-dependent on the subject. As a counter-argument to this conviction can be cited the fact of (e.g. visionary) hallucination in which the subject cognizing it is also convinced that the source of its existence lies in something outside him and even has the same conviction that he perceives some (transcendent) thing outside the realm of his being as a man in fact perceiving a certain thing. And the hallucination proves to be resistant to attempts to get rid of it by the exertion of consciousness alone and against attempts to change it by acts of consciousness. But there are means enabling the subject to distinguish between hallucinations and the sense data cognized during "normal" perception of some thing simply by the fact of the difference between the data of hallucination and the data of perception which somehow show themselves to be "stronger" than hallucination and lead to devaluation of their reality by pushing them somehow down to the level of "a simple appearance." Furthermore, there are also ways of recognizing that these hallucinations (which do not really have the source of their existence in any object remaining entirely outside the limits of the being of the hallucinating subject (that is, in some material thing – as it occurs after the constitution of a full perception in which this thing is given)) nevertheless have a source in an object which is different from the stream of consciousness of the hallucinating subject, although it is "bound" to this subject in his morbid state. We are entitled to point out this fact as Husserl also takes into account in his investigations the so-called *Leibgegebenheit* (the mode of givenness of the subject's own body to him) and the role of the constituted body in the course of perceptive experience concerning things and processes of the environing world. These links between the phenomenon of hallucination and certain processes or states of the body (in the sense of *Leib*) is at the same time closely connected with a certain resistance of this phenomenon against attempts to get rid of it by the hallucinating subject. In both cases – the case of cognized sense data on whose basis we perceive things and the case of hallucination which invokes in the hallucinating person the conviction of the presence of some reality outside him – the character of something other (not created by acts of consciousness and independent of them to a certain extent) explains the fact that in the process of cognitive perception there arises in the constitution of the object sense of a certain thing (or process), a sense pointing to an existential autonomy of this thing (i.e. existing "in itself"). Similarly with the "sense" data sometimes called "deep impressions," data localized in our body as e.g. impressions of muscles, joints, toothache or headache[17] which also have this special character of something which invades the subject as something already there and alien to his Ego and to a certain degree in its existence and qualities of a character independent of purely conscious operations of the subject.

Independently of our will we feel a toothache in certain circumstances or one pleasure or another and we can have influence on whether and how we know such data, finally only through a certain change in our bodily behavior. The exclusive conscious behavior is insufficient. And, as in the previously mentioned cases, this character of something already there and alien to the subject and resistant to a certain extent to the purely conscious behavior of the subject has as a consequence in the course of cognition of our own body that there occurs the cognition as

---

[17] We call them so in everyday life and also in psychology which understands them as psychic "states" caused by physiological processes. Here – where we do purely phenomenological investigations without making use of the premise of the natural existence of the world and the existence in this world of a certain particular material object called "our body" – we can take the process of internal sense data in their purely phenomenal character as a basis for a particular experiential cognition of our own body, cognition in which something "constitutes itself" as "my body." Such phenomena exist without doubt and play a quite special role in the cognition of "my own body" as the object which finally becomes known as something existing "objectively" in the real world, i.e. autonomously in relation to our previous cognition.

though of something which – although it is connected with us in a specific way such that we cannot do without it in the limits of our life – is at the same time autonomous in its being in relation to the acts of consciousness cognizing the body and is in the same way "in itself" as are things in the environing world. Being still at the introductory stage of the constitutive investigation we cannot say that the process of creating synthetic object sense takes place "exclusively" due to separate conscious behavior of the perceiving subject. But when we go over to the high levels of the constitutive process then there, also, as I said, we meet with a remarkable difference between the purely receptive, adaptive behavior of the subject and the creative and productive behavior. In both cases their result may be the constituting of a certain object sense as something which is produced by the conscious subject and this would not occur if the corresponding conscious processes did not take place, carried out by the perceiving subject and on the basis of perception cognizing a certain reality in the limits of the environing real world. Nevertheless, in every one of the opposing cases the course of further cognition of the given thing is different. Where there are at play expressively productive acts of consciousness of the cognitive subject the same subject in further cognition obtains as if a distrust of the object sense created by him which, although this latter may have in its content a moment denoting the autonomous being of the object of the given sense, undermines the weight of the moment and in consequence excludes from the cognitive process all the moments or elements of the object sense which grows from this "creative" conscious behavior of the subject. This exclusion entails that in consequence of this the object appearing through this object sense, "undermined" in its weight as to at least some moments, is not recognized by the cognitive subject as existing autonomously or possessing autonomous qualities which appear through these questioned moments of the object sense. But the matter looks quite otherwise in the case when the perceiving subject in the constitutive process behaves primarily receptively and adapts to the experienced data or to adumbrations built on them when he tries only to understand what groups, sets of original data supply. By adapting and behaving receptively, may be in a very active way, there arises the creation of an object sense which is not "exclusively" the production of his own free and conscious behavior, but is produced under the impact of a reality imposing itself on him and independent of him. This still does not in itself settle whether this reality is in all its autonomous qualities accurately such as it is finally given in perception leading to the final cognitive effect. The fact that a certain thing is given to the perceiving subject in a certain set of intuitive qualities does not guarantee that this mode of givenness is in every respect the right cognitively binding one. But this entire process assumes one thing, namely, that in the production of the object sense there also participates some entity different in its existence and qualities from the perceiving subject and that, therefore, it is not only permissible but also necessary to draw distinctions between the constituted object sense and the object which appears more or less truthfully through this same sense, or corresponds to it or at least is something alien, independent in its being, from the conscious acts of the subject. If it is only possible and necessary to make this distinction regardless of the object sense obtained in a certain process of perception of the thing revealing truthfully or not the mode of existence and qualities of the thing, it is impossible to say that the very production of this synthetic object sense leads to the creation of the object in this appearing sense and that this object in its existence is existentially derivative and existentially dependent on the behavior of consciousness of the perceiving subject. But only if we had the right to say this would the solution in favor of transcendental idealism be justified.

Of course, all this investigation is very abbreviated and should be developed with the help of sufficiently explicated constitutive investigations. But the topics inquired into here seem to be sufficient for the aims of the argument which I am conducting here.

f) My investigations give, indeed, the basis for the appropriate answer to the Husserlian results treated in the first part of this essay under f). And it is necessary to inquire in the course of the constitutive analysis whether e.g. the conditions necessary for the constitution of certain unity of sense in some constitutive layer (on the basis of a certain definite set of noematic senses of the lower layer) are at the same time sufficient – thanks to the

appropriate behavior of the cognitive subject[18] – for the constitution of this unity or if there is also needed "active," "creative" behavior of the subject not taking experience into account.
Only in this latter case is it possible to agree that the creation of
the synthetic sense of the higher constitutive layer and finally the
sense of the perceived object is a production *sine fundamento in re*
and only if this would have to take place in e v e r y case of constitution is it possible to agree that the produced sense in general
cannot have anything in common with the autonomous qualities
of the object which in the given cognitive process is to become
known, i.e. to agree that this sense can be false. But this would
not entitle us to say that only intentional objects can be recognized as existing f o r the cognitive subject and reject the object
existing "in itself" and eventually "for itself."

Husserl might answer that if it was possible to show that such
"creative" behavior of the cognitive subject is unavoidably
necessary[19] and that, accordingly, the object, allegedly existing
autonomously, not only is not known but is in its essence unknowable, then we would have to agree that there is no ground
for accepting the existence in this mode of essentially unknowable
objects and that – reasonably enough – we have to limit ourselves
to recognize objects which are nothing else and "nothing more"
than constituted object senses (purely intentional objects). Just
as Kant had insufficient grounds for accepting "things in themselves" and had to limit himself to the recognition of "phenomena"
then here we have to reject – Husserl would say – the allegedly
autonomously existing objects and content ourselves with the
recognition of intentional correlates of sets of cognitive acts.

It has to be asserted that Husserl, in his works hitherto
known to us, did not show that there essentially and constantly
occurs this extremely "creative" process in the constitution of
object senses. His idealist thesis is, then, insufficiently substan-

[18] By "appropriate" behavior is meant behavior in which the cognitive subject
endeavors to make clear to himself the contents of the noematic senses of the lower
layer and by creating synthetic sense of the higher layer adapt to the contents of the
set of experiences of the lower layer and at the same time as far as possible to exclude
not only the erroneous apprehension of the experienced senses but also, as I said above,
the consequences of the "creative" transgression beyond what the content of the
senses of the lower constitutive layer suggests.

[19] As it is, according to Kant, unavoidably necessary to apprehend known objects
in *a priori* categorial forms and time and space as forms of intuition (*Anschauungs-
formen*).

tiated by the results of his analyses. Secondly, we have to agree
that if it were proved that some object from its own essence had
necessarily to be unknowable, at first sight, we would have no
grounds for accepting its existence. But this is not necessary. On
what basis would we have the right to assert of this essence that
it excludes its cognition? Would not such an assertion presuppose
that we know this essence and that it is not unknowable at all?
But if we say that not from its essence but from the essence of
our cognitive acts it becomes unknowable then we have, firstly,
to show that this is not only from the essence of our cognitive
operations but that from the essence of all possible cognitive
operations the object becomes unknowable. If only the first case
occurred we should have no ground for asserting that this object is
really unknowable because whether or not it was such for us
it would not be such for whatever other type of cognitive subjects. If we referred this relative unknowability to the object
existing autonomously then we would not have the right to assert
that its very concept is deprived of reasonable sense, but only
that we had not succeeded, maybe even for some reasons necessarily inherent in our nature, in cognizing such objects. Our
cognitive operations would then, but probably unjustly, be recognized as "cognitive." In the second case, there would be no
grounds for arguing that these in their essence did not lead to any
knowledge of objects autonomously existing, nor would there be
grounds for excluding the possibility of taking what was cognitive
as merely deceptive. In any case, we would have to take rather
the agnostic position but not decide to adopt the idealist solution
recognizing at the same time the realist solution as permissible
although it can be out of our reach.

But Husserl would reply: Exactly from the special "thetic"
function emerges the idea of, for example, the "autonomous"
being independent of our acts of consciousness and, particularly,
of these "thetic" acts which create the whole of our experience.
They give without justification the sense of an autonomous being
to phenomena which are only intentional, that is, existentially
heteronomous.

Let us agree that this character of autonomous existence (in
particular the real) is "given" to certain object senses due to the
performance of correspondingly structured "thetic" acts, that

this character becomes correlative to these acts. But only correlative? And is this kind of "sense giving" essentially unjustifiably carried out in regard to the existential character of certain objects which we cognize or even all? What entitles us to assert this groundlessness? What entitles us to the proposition that if something appears in the wake of the performance of certain cognitive (let us say "thetic") acts then this *ipso facto* must necessarily be only the intentional correlate of these acts but not something that was disclosed through these acts? Would it not be surprising that acts in which, often after a long deliberation after having performed a series of perceptive operations obtained on the basis of results acquired by experiments organized by us, we, finally, come to the conviction that in any case some such thing exists as these cognitive acts in their contents teach us that these acts were in their essence to be the source of such an unbelievable delusion actually depriving our acts and cognitive operations of every sense and also the sense of many, if not all, of our practical activities creating the seeming deception of autonomous existence where it in reality is not. And *cui bono*? Maybe, our moral life, as Fichte would have it, could be realized on this basis? Or, maybe, on the contrary not more justified – due to the "constitutive" contemplation – is the assertion that if thetic acts give to objects such a sense of existence in the cognized experience then this springs from the fact that the cognitive subject is inclined to this by the existential character of "otherness" and independence (resistance) of the primary sense data and in general of certain compulsory consequence in the subject in the course of the constitution to which the subject must adapt when he truly longs for understanding and apprehension of what he deals with. This is naturally not a sufficient decision to take a "realist" position against Husserl, this is rather pointing in the direction in which we could express not only the lack of conviction in the correctness of Husserl's basic theses but also assert that there exists sufficient ground for accepting positively the existential autonomy of the real world given to us in experience. But there is still a long way to go to reach this goal.

4. CRITICAL REMARKS ON THE FORMAL-ONTOLOGICAL
SOURCES OF THE HUSSERLIAN IDEALISM

Finally, let us consider the formal and material ontological arguments which may lead to the idealist solution. This is, I remind you, the thesis about the transcendence of real objects, particularly perceived objects, in relation to cognitive acts in which they are given, and, secondly, the assertion about the fundamental material difference between spatial (material-physical) things and conscious experiences and, at last, the application of these two propositions to the problem of the existential connection which is to hold between pure consciousness and real objects, a connection which appears in two different cases: a) the relation between consciousness and "body" (*Leib*) of the experiencing subject, b) the relation between the perceived object and perception. These two cases state that when they occur, the pure consciousness becomes somehow an element of the real world (as we, men, belong to this world). Apparent objections to this are the above-mentioned ontological propositions and one further formal-ontological proposition expressly held by Husserl, namely, that only what remains in relation to something else, emanating from its essence, can create a uniform whole of one object along with this other "object." Both transcendence and the radical difference emanating from its essence compared with consciousness (particularly outer perception) excludes, on the cited formal-ontological premise, the creation of a unity of one object through the relation between a perceived (physical, spatial) object and the process of perception. On this level of contact with reality there cannot occur an inclusion of pure consciousness in the real world, this inclusion would be possible only when we denied the existential autonomous character of perceived objects and made them – in line with Husserl's idealist solution – only noematic object senses necessarily intentionally denoted by synthetically, uniformly connected acts of experience. Still more impossible seems – on the basis of the given premises – the acceptance of a close relation between pure consciousness and the body (e.g. the nervous system) of the experiencing subject, which would lead to an essentially uniform compact whole: the soul-bodied consciously experiencing man. And here the hiatus of the material essence between what is conscious and what is bodily excludes this kind of unity. But if our body is nothing other than a certain intentionally denoted object sense then, from this point of view, it can belong as intentional correlate to a uniform stream of pure consciousness and the whole of reality would not break up in two alien and unconnectable hemispheres of individual being: pure consciousness and the material (physico-spatial) world.

Can we deny any of the premises on which the idealist solution is based? Can we throw out the transcendence of the real physical object and perception? All the analyses of sense perception and other cognitive acts concerning material things (from the cognitive side) compel us to accept this thesis. All suppositions – not foreign to idealism, that of Berkeley, for instance – that the perceived thing is somehow immanent in our perception, seem to be preposterous, not taking into account especially the formal-ontological structure of physical things and the essence of the experiences of consciousness. Can we reject the formal-ontological proposition that that and only that can belong to the unity of the individual object which is in its essence related to the other elements appearing in the same object or to its inseparate moments? This assertion Husserl nowhere justifies – as far as I know.[20] And at least at first sight this assertion seems intuitively evident. Why should it be possible to maintain the object's unity and whole if it was not grounded in the inner contents of its own essence? However, it is possible to doubt if it is really an entirely general proposition although as a formal-ontological one in the Husserlian sense[21] it should be so. But my investigations in

[20] At least he does not justify it in *Ideas I* where he explicitly states it.
[21] Husserl's concept of formal ontology is different from the manner in which I tried to understand this philosophical discipline. I based my theory on a concept, to be distinguished from other concepts, of the "categorial form" of an object (a form which can differ according to the different types of things that exist, e.g. individual objects, intentional objects, ideas, relations etc.). But Husserl comes to the concept of formal ontology just by setting forth the concept of an "object" (something) in general with the widest range of this generality and reaches it by comprehensive variation of all the object's determinations. From this it would follow that formal-ontological propositions *eo ipso* must adapt themselves to everything that exists. And L. Landgrebe, when he many years ago read my work *Über den formalen Aufbau des individuellen Gegenstandes* (*Studia Philosophica*, vol. 1, Leopoli 1935) informed me that it cannot be included in formal ontology as it is not sufficiently general. He used then, of course, Husserl's concept of formal ontology as the "most general" of all the sciences. He told me about this when I met him in January 1936 when I visited Husserl.

the *Controversy about the Existence of the World*[22] on the formally different objects, among others the "essence" of the individual object and various fundamental varieties of this essence, compel us to be cautious. One may surmise that Husserl's proposition is true only in relation to some objects, namely, to the individual, autonomous objects with radical or eventually exact essence[23]; whether it is valid for the remaining types of autonomous objects seems to be doubtful. In any case, this whole matter demands detailed analysis in two directions. First, concerning to what extent the investigated formal-ontological proposition refers to different types of objects as concerns the formal structure of their essence and, second, concerning the type of objects in this respect to which, on the one hand, pure consciousness belongs – taken as consciousness in general without regard to its variations such as, e.g., perception or thought or any other, e.g., emotional acts – and, on the other hand, physical things. It must not be forgotten that among these things we have, on the one hand, inanimate things but, on the other, different kinds of organisms. It is far from evident that e.g. all bodily (physical) objects behave in the same manner and it can be conjectured that here not only spatiality (as would emerge from Husserl's remarks on this theme, uncritically following the distinctions and traditions e.g. of Cartesianism) plays its role but also different kinds of organization of the internal structure of the given physical body (from totally unorganized gases through liquids, crystals – through the solid bodies *sensu stricto* – to the highly organized organisms, particularly the human body). It is not excluded that in these different cases we have objects whose essence has a different formal structure and that, consequently, the fact of their falling under the formal ontological proposition considered here can be stated only after this matter has been investigated.

In this connection it seems to be an unsolved question what is the type of essence, on the one hand, of pure consciousness and physical things (of various types) on the other. Husserl speaks in a too schematic manner about the opposition between the real objects (the transcendent ones in relation to consciousness, and

---

[22] Cf. *l.c.*, Chapter XIV, "Essence of the individual autonomous object," p. 202–272, vol. II (2nd ed.).
[23] Cf. *l.c.*, p. 240 fn.

in particular to conscious cognitive acts in which these realia are cognized) but in any case first and foremost under the aspect of difference as to the manner in which they are given directly in cognition: the ones in immanent perception, not through adumbrations, the others in transcendent perceptions appearing in a complicated system of adumbrations of different types and stages. Concerning this cognitive aspect of the difference between the contrasted essences Husserl can be considered to be right. But his results concerning the difference between the material essence of consciousness and different types of physical objects are not adequate to the same extent. To limit oneself to the opposition between spatiality and non-spatiality is not satisfactory, and this opposition – as Max Scheler once remarked – demands a certain revision. In any case, more eidetic research has to be done in this respect in order to be able to solve the problem whether the difference of essences of the objects concerned is really so deep that any form of a symbiosis, as it were, is excluded between consciousness and the body (NB of the organized type). At the stage of development of knowledge which Husserl represents in his *Ideas* it is not possible, in my opinion, to solve this problem and his verdict in this matter seems at least to be unjustified.

But one other question must be considered here. There can be two different cases of "relation" between consciousness and the real world: a) in the case of a cognitive relation between the cognitive subject, in particular the perceiving one, and the perceived body, b) in the case of "relation" between consciousness and body (*Leib*) of the perceiving subject or experiencing in general. In the first case there is, of course, no possibility of creating one object (out of perception and the perceived body) and there is no need that such a unity should be created. They must remain two mutually transcendent entities. Only it can be asked what kind of relation between them must be in order that it be sufficient and indispensable for the possibility of obtaining knowledge about the perceived object by the perceiving subject. Naturalists, and in particular psycho-physiologists, demand that this relation in which "experience" is to appear in the perceiving subject be causal. We cannot decide here if this is really so, or if we can satisfy ourselves with some other kind of relation or if the causal relation is here sufficient for acquiring knowledge by the

subject about some physical thing or about some other psycho-
physical object (about other people). Are we compelled to postulate, if this relation is to occur, so far-reaching a similarity or
affinity between the essences of these objects that they would have
to create some objective unity if not some kind of one compact
object? This seems doubtful but demands, of course, a special
investigation which we do not find in Husserl. A matter undoubtedly more complicated is the problem of the "relation" between
consciousness and the organic body with which, as I think, it is
connected. Here there can be some kind of such a relation that
the whole creates one object. But the problem of the relations
between "soul and body – which is as old as European philosophy
– has not been solved by Husserl and was not, in my opinion,
taken by him even one step beyond the traditional state of the
problem in spite of undoubted progress in the research on the
so-called "givenness of the body" (Husserl's *Leibgegebenheit*). It is
not to be solved so rapidly as some people imagine it might be. But
research on this must continue and not without importance will
certainly be the results obtained in this field by theoretical
biology which may be able to obtain a better insight into the
eidetic phenomenological problems of the whole matter.

This whole argument, the raising of which could have had influence on Husserl's idealist solution, seems to me to be insufficiently mature so that, essentially, it would be permissible
to try to solve it or, rather, avoid it through the idealist solution
in the form in which we find it in Husserl. If Husserl's work on
the problems leads to his adoption of transcendental idealism then
it seems to me that this is an untimely solution before which it is
necessary to be able to appeal to further research both in the field
of ontology and the empirical-natural sciences whose results
cannot be dogmatically presupposed but whose heuristic role
must not be neglected.

In the end of these undoubtedly sketchy considerations on the
grounds for Husserl's transcendental idealism it has to be declared,
I think, that – in so far as I am right in saying that this idealism
was derived from the sources to which I pointed – the arguments
I have scrutinized are either unsatisfactory or even quite wrong.
Some other arguments have to be found if Husserl's position is to

be defended. Further research in all the directions I have indicated is certainly necessary. It is not sufficient to have only sufficient ground for rejecting Husserl's solution but it must also be possible to have sufficiently clarified some other theory about the mode of existence of the real world and its existential relation to consciousness in which its cognition takes place and also to have at our disposal appropriate arguments for its justification. But this has to be attempted in a purely systematic contemplation. I tried to take the first steps in the *Controversy about the Existence of the World*.

Paris 1960, Cracow 1962

INDEX